# Prosper

### ENJOYING
### INTIMACY WITH GOD

# Prosper

## ENJOYING INTIMACY WITH GOD

NATE BRAMSEN

**PROSPER:**
**ENJOYING INTIMACY WITH GOD**
By Nate Bramsen

Copyright © 2021 ROCK International
Printed in the United States of America

**ISBN-13: 978-1-62041-011-0**

**R**elief, **O**pportunity & **C**are for **K**ids • www.rockintl.org
**R**esources **O**f **C**rucial **K**nowledge • www.king-of-glory.com
P.O. Box 4766, Greenville, SC 29608 USA
resources@rockintl.org

Cover design by Vinay Mathews

To my daughter,
*Haven Rahab*

---

My prayer has always been that you would love
the *Word of God* and the *God of the Word*.

May you be one who truly prospers—
*not* as the world defines prosperity,
but as *God* declares true prosperity to be.

This is my prayer for you.
May you be able to say,
*"My soul keeps your testimonies;*
*I love them exceedingly."*
(Psalm 119:167)

---

# Table of Contents

## It was September 21, 2018...

Ten days earlier, my wife and I had welcomed the news that our first child was on the way. Our joy, anticipation, and gratitude were palpable.

But now I was in Wichita, Kansas, speaking at a school. My phone rang. The message conveyed by the voice on the other end was succinct and direct: **"You have cancer."**

In a moment's time, I found myself at the crossroads of decision. I needed to determine, then and there, whether I would resist this news and think of it as an inconvenience and a disruption to my plans or whether I would accept it as a welcome invitation toward deeper intimacy with the God who had made me for Himself. **Could it be that this reconstruction of my plans was actually an answer to my heart-prayer, *"That I may know him!"*** (Philippians 3:10)?

Psalm 1:2-3 blessed, challenged, and encouraged my soul during those days of cancer, radiation, and isolation. Originally posted as a YouTube series in March of 2019 (during the isolation of radioactive iodine treatment), the following pages are a journey through those two verses. In them we will find a blessed invitation extended by God to each of us to "Come and *truly* prosper by My stream."

God isn't looking for those who merely obey His precepts; His deep desire is a people who delight in His Person. He longs for us to *taste and see that the Lord is **good*** (Psalm 34:8). He is waiting for us to enter into the fullness of His love so that we might come to know the fulfillment of that verse: *"**Blessed** is the man who takes refuge in Him!"*

My prayer over this book is that:

> **It will be a catalyst which will spur this generation to intimately and personally love the *Word of God* and the *God of the Word*.**
>
> **The goal of this journey is not to know more *about* God; it is, rather, to better know *God*.**

As you read these chapters, I urge you to take in the content slowly, humbly, and prayerfully. Take time to journal your responses to the questions, to pray through any convictions God's Spirit impresses on your heart, and to actively allow Him to recalibrate your understanding of His love and of your life. The invitation to *prosper* is not some ambiguous idea in Scripture; it is a Divine appeal, made to all, and realized by each one who sincerely responds. *"The people who know their God shall stand firm and take action"* (Daniel 11:32).

— *Nate Bramsen*

## THE *Passion* OF THE BLESSED MAN

**PSALM 1:1-3** *Blessed is the man who walks not in the counsel of the wicked, nor stands in the way of sinners, nor sits in the seat of scoffers; but **his delight is in the law of the Lord**, and on His law he meditates day and night. He is like a tree planted by streams of water that yields its fruit in its season, and its leaf does not wither. In all that he does, he prospers.*

**BIG IDEA:**

THE SOURCE OF OUR DELIGHT WILL OFTEN DETERMINE OUR STABILITY IN LIFE. WHEN OUR JOY IS EBBING, IT IS A SOLID INDICATOR THAT OUR CIRCUMSTANCES HAVE DISTRACTED US FROM OUR TRUE **PASSION**.

Turn your focus to one line from Psalm 1:2. *"His delight is in the law of the Lord."* The first word we want to target is this *delight*, or this **passion**, of the blessed man. Here, we're given a glimpse of the heart of one whose drive is to know God intimately. But what does that journey into deeper intimacy with God look like? Where does it begin?

*The source of our delight* will often determine our level of stability. Find an unstable person, and you will find an unstable, or unreliable, source of delight. But is it right to say that *delight* and *passion* are synonymous here?

**THE SOURCE OF OUR DELIGHT WILL OFTEN DETERMINE OUR LEVEL OF STABILITY.** The kind of delight the psalmist speaks of conveys two important factors which link it clearly to passion. First, we see that this delight drives "the blessed man" to action, and second, this delight is something for which he is willing to suffer (which we will discuss in detail later). The word *passion* comes from the

Latin word *pati*, meaning "suffering". (This helps us to understand why the week of Easter is also called Passion Week; it is a week set aside to remember Christ's suffering on our behalf.)

We might think that such a concept of suffering for delight is foreign to our day, but consider these examples:

- The sweat and pain of athletics
- The rigorous intensity of academics
- The meticulous attention and numerous hours given to perfecting an art
- The jostling of political candidates to garner votes
- The compelling preoccupation and impressive undertakings to gain someone's affection
- The extensive efforts employed in pursuing a promotion

We can undoubtedly say that there is much *suffering* involved in the pursuit of one's *delight.*

It seems obvious, then, that this true delight spoken of in Psalm 1 is not a mere feeling. Feelings fluctuate. Take a moment to take hold of this truth. The delight of the blessed man will not ever be found anywhere within his circumstances. People change, relationships change, teams change, careers change, leaders change, nations change—*but God's Word is constant!* Because of this, true delight—delight in the law of the Lord—stands on a firm and fixed foundation. Consider the words of Jesus Christ: *"Heaven and earth will pass away, but My words will not pass away"* (Luke 21:33). And Peter reminds us, *"The grass withers, and the flower falls, but the word of the Lord remains forever"* (1 Peter 1:24-25).

We must allow this truth to penetrate our understanding. Circumstances have *nothing* to do with the blessedness of the man in Psalm 1. **When our foundation is secure, joy can control our attitude even when our preferences, our expectations, and our feelings alter or even when they are ripped away by circumstances.** If this were not the case, how could we possibly obey God's imperative to us to *"rejoice in the Lord always"* (Philippians 4:4)?

Whenever my joy *does* fluctuate, I need to ask myself, "On what or on whom was I basing my joy? What was I truly rejoicing in?" Remember, Philippians 4:3 precedes Philippians 4:4. Profound, I know! But the command in Philippians 4:4 to *"rejoice in the Lord always; again I will say, rejoice,"* is preceded by Paul's declaration to his readers and listeners that their names are written in the Book of Life; they are enrolled in heaven. They have eternal life. Their foundation goes far deeper than their present circumstances.

We commit a great injustice when we define *rejoicing* simply as smiles, laughter, and pleasant things. That is not biblical rejoicing. The key to rejoicing is found in the phrase, *"Rejoice in the Lord"* (Philippians 4:4). Don't be deceived: external, emotional happiness, or the lack thereof, is not a reliable indicator of true, godly rejoicing. Time and again, Christ wept, mourned, and grieved. He was called *"a man of sorrows and acquainted with grief"* (Isaiah 53:3). Yet we know that the Lord Jesus never did anything outside His Father's will. No, true delight does not reel with the fluctuations of the physical—our body, our environment, our circumstances. True delight finds a resting place in *"the law of the Lord."*

Be encouraged by this warning:

**When our joy is ebbing, let it be a quick reminder to us that we've become distracted by our surroundings and have shifted our focus from the true passion, the blessed man's passion.** Our height of rejoicing is a touchstone of the health of our passion. The Psalm 1 man knows his passion. His delight is in God's truth, *"the law of the Lord."* This law is an immutable Truth: culture cannot change it, ideologies cannot infiltrate it, and circumstances cannot conquer it. Though we like to blame our circumstances, they are not the root of the problem when it comes to the pursuit of a blessed life; they are not the obstacle which stands in our way. Rather, it is our passion. And so we must re-evaluate often to assess where our true passion lies.

The reality is this: The circumstances in which you find yourself are perfectly suited for you to fully glorify God. Perhaps some of your choices thus far have been far from perfect. Perhaps the consequences of those sinful choices have left an unwelcome imprint on the present. Still, the sweet truth of God's ways remains unchanged, so I'll say it again: **The circumstances in which you find yourself are perfectly suited for you to fully glorify God.**

The exemplary man of Psalm 1 is not *choosing* blessedness as an option; he is *finding* blessedness as an outcome of his delight, his passion. And why? His delight is in that which cannot be touched by earthly discouragements, devices, dissensions, disillusionments, or divisions—it is in the eternal, immutable Law of the Lord. When you choose to truly delight in God's way, blessing will be your constant journeying companion.

**A TIME FOR**

*Reflection*

**SELF-EXAMINATION:** What's driving your heart today? Does your joy (not happiness) sway according to circumstances—a doctor's report, a job evaluation, a message received, a political shake-up—which threaten to distract? Have you shifted your focus away from that which never changes? This question is not asked in a spirit of condemnation, but rather to offer an invitation—an invitation to dig deeply down to the source that never changes and to lay the whole of your delight, your passion, there, in that one place where you are loved with an everlasting love, where you are invited into an intimate relationship with the true and living God, and where you can fulfill the eternal purpose for which you were created.

> *From the breaking of the dawn to the setting of the sun,*
> *I will stand on ev'ry promise of Your Word.*
> *Words of power, strong to save, that will never pass away,*
> *I will stand on ev'ry promise of Your Word.*
> *For Your covenant is sure,*
> *And on this I am secure,*
> *I can stand on ev'ry promise of Your Word.[1]*

**QUESTIONS TO CONSIDER:** Before addressing these questions, take a few minutes to write down your initial thoughts and reactions to this chapter. What stands out to you? What questions come to mind? What does your flesh initially want to resist?

1. What (life event, relationship, feeling, etc.) causes your joy to fluctuate? In what ways would that area of life look different if it were surrendered to *"the law of the Lord"*?

2. What circumstances do you view as *obstacles to* blessing rather than *opportunities for* blessing?

3. Do you agree or disagree with this statement? **"The circumstances in which you find yourself are perfectly suited for you to fully glorify God."** Give a reason for your answer.

4. How do your passions line up with what Christ is passionate about?

5. In a world of constant change, how would you define *stability*? Is your concept of this word in line with this psalm? Why or why not?

6. What choices are you willing to make to combat spiritual instability?

7. What was Christ willing to suffer for? What are you truly willing to suffer for? (Give examples.)

# Notes

# THE *Prosperity* OF THE BLESSED MAN

**PSALM 1:1-3** *Blessed is the man who walks not in the counsel of the wicked, nor stands in the way of sinners, nor sits in the seat of scoffers; but **his delight is in the law of the Lord**, and on His law he meditates day and night. He is like a tree planted by streams of water that yields its fruit in its season, and its leaf does not wither. In all that he does, he prospers.*

**BIG IDEA:**

BIBLICAL **PROSPERITY** IS FOUND IN INTIMACY WITH CHRIST RATHER THAN IN THE ABUNDANCE OF POSSESSIONS.

As we continue our exploration into these few verses which start the book of Psalms, keep in mind this thought: Our journey is primarily about knowing God more, not knowing more about God. It is about intimacy with God and enjoying that intimacy with Him.

Turn your attention once again to this singular phrase in verse two: *"His delight is in the law of the Lord."* Here we see true **prosperity**—the prosperity of the blessed man. Now, before you bring any preconceived notion to the table, it's only fair that you be warned: We will be travelling in the opposite direction to much of what is said today on the topic of biblical prosperity.

The Hebrew language has a couple of words for *delight*. One of these words does express the idea of a happiness that makes us want to dance and party. But, as we've already discussed, the particular form of *delight* used in Psalm 1 speaks of a passion and, even greater, a passion that is willing to suffer. Let's look more closely at this word.

The Hebrew word is *chephets*, but what does it mean? It actually conveys the concept of great value. To quote Tim Keller, "This word *delight* literally means 'to feel rich'."[2]

To understand the implications of this word, take a look at another usage of *chephets* in Proverbs 3:13-15. It reads, *"Blessed is the one who finds wisdom, and the one who gets understanding, for the gain from her is better than gain from silver and her profit better than gold. She is more precious than jewels, and nothing you **desire*** (that's our word, translated as *delight* in Psalm 1:2) *can compare with her."*

**The blessed man in Psalm 1 did not prosper in the plenitude of possessions, in his own physical prowess, or in political power. Only the sweet savor derived from meditating on God's Word, soaking in God's law, and coming to know the heart of his God brought him into the blessings of true prosperity.** Even in Psalm 1:3 we are told, *"In all that he does, he prospers."* It only makes sense then that the psalmist writes in Psalm 19:10, speaking of the same law of God, *"More to be **desired** are they* [just decrees] *than gold, even much fine gold, sweeter also than honey and the drippings of the honeycomb."*

> ONLY THE SWEET SAVOR DERIVED FROM MEDITATING ON GOD'S WORD, SOAKING IN GOD'S LAW, AND COMING TO KNOW THE HEART OF HIS GOD BROUGHT HIM INTO THE BLESSINGS OF **TRUE PROSPERITY**

How do you define *prosperity*? Good health? A solid portfolio? A happy, easy life? Many friends? Or, perhaps, intimacy with God?

As a cancer patient, I would often hear the term "beating cancer." For me, beating cancer would not be defined as the removal of malignant cells gone wild. Rather, it would mean, above all else, knowing and cherishing Christ more through it all. In fact, if I were to be declared "cancer-free" without ever knowing Christ more intimately, I would consider it loss. In Paul's words, *"Indeed, I count everything as loss because of the surpassing worth of knowing Christ Jesus my Lord. For His sake I have suffered the loss of all things and count them as rubbish, in order that I may gain Christ"* (Philippians 3:8). But don't be discouraged if you did not experience victory in past circumstances entrusted to you. Remember, God does much more than forgive our broken past. He redeems it!

**GOD DOES MUCH MORE THAN FORGIVE OUR BROKEN PAST. HE REDEEMS IT!**

Perhaps you need to pray today for a transformation of perspective on what constitutes true value, true prosperity. According to God's definition, the individual who seeks first the things of this world is not rich. **Sure, we may prosper in the things of this world, but they will not last. And worse, the rich treasures of God's wealth will remain before us, unmined, because we have failed—even refused—to excavate their depths. Our faith will grow weak as the "riches" we have chosen prove inferior and unsatisfactory.**

Are you prospering in ways that do not actually matter? As John prayed for Gaius, *"Beloved, I pray that you may prosper in all things and be in health, just as your soul prospers"* (3 John v.2 NKJV). I pray the same for you, my friend. May you be prosperous—in all that truly matters.

**SELF-EXAMINATION:** The ultimate goal is to know Christ and to glorify Him in the midst of our situation, so let's ask ourselves a few questions to that end. What does "financial prosperity" look like from an eternal perspective? Would it be defined as being wealthy or being generous? How about "relational prosperity"? To be famous or faithful? And what about "physical prosperity"—prospering in our physical bodies? Is it to be physically healthy or spiritually holy? **In considering cancer, I'd suggest that neither a doctor's declaration of being cancer-free nor walking through death's door has any bearing at all on whether or not victory has been won.** After all, death is not the final word for a believer in Jesus Christ. Instead, death for us means the resurrection and being forever with the Lord.

A TIME FOR

*Reflection*

In light of this, maybe the question we should be asking as we evaluate any circumstance is this: "Is Jesus Christ being made known and glorified?" Intimacy with God—that is true prosperity. Thus, when our ultimate delight is in the "law of the Lord," our life will prosper, regardless of man's evaluation.

> *But we never can prove the delights of His love / Until all on the altar we lay;*
> *For the favor He shows, for the joy He bestows / Are for them who will trust and obey.*[3]

**QUESTIONS TO CONSIDER:** Before addressing these questions, take a few minutes to write down your initial thoughts and reactions to this chapter. What stands out to you? What questions come to mind? What does your flesh initially want to resist?

1. How do you define *prosperity*? How does your definition differ from the definition revealed in God's Word?

2. Is there an area of your life where you consider yourself to be prospering, yet, according to this psalm, you're actually living in poverty of spirit?

3. How does Christ define *prosperity*? Provide Scripture references to back up your definition.

4. What does prospering look like in your day-to-day life—from an eternal perspective?

5. Reflect on a circumstance when maybe you didn't attain to the world's definition of success but in which you were still able to prosper.

6. Reflect on a circumstance that you see as waste but which, if given to God, He will still redeem. How might it look to allow past hurt and disappointment to be used for God's glory?

7. How can we know God and glorify Him in the mundane day-to-day?

# Notes

# THE *Polarization* OF THE BLESSED MAN

**PSALM 1:1-3** *Blessed is the man who walks not in the counsel of the wicked, nor stands in the way of sinners, nor sits in the seat of scoffers; but his delight is in the law of the Lord, and on His law he meditates day and night. He is like a tree planted by streams of water that yields its fruit in its season, and its leaf does not wither. In all that he does, he prospers.*

**BIG IDEA:**

LIVING A **POLARIZED** LIFE ISN'T A DECISION TO WALK AWAY FROM THE WORLD, BUT A DETERMINATION TO WALK DECIDEDLY IN THE WORD.

One small key word at the beginning of Psalm 1:2 launches us into the psalmist's desired trajectory.

**But.**

*"But his delight is in the law of the Lord."* This conjunction sets the stage for some monumental statements in the Word of God: *"For the wages of sin is death, **but** the free gift of God is eternal life in Christ Jesus our Lord"* (Romans 6:23). *"**But** now in Christ Jesus you who once were far off have been brought near by the blood of Christ"* (Ephesians 2:13). This word in Psalm 1 is no different. It changes everything.

Look at the **polarization** of the blessed man. Lexico defines *polarization* as a "division into two sharply contrasting groups or sets of opinions or beliefs." At the one extreme, or pole, we read in Psalm 1:1 of the progressive downward slide of the perishing: a slow, slippery slope of sin which started with walking *("walks...in the counsel of the wicked")*, slowed to standing ("*stands in the way of sinners*"), and stopped at sitting ("*sits in the seat of scoffers*"). This is the path of the one who receives advice from the world without allowing it to first pass through the filter of verse 2 ("*but his delight is in the law of the Lord*").

These individuals are after three things: abundance for self, approval from others, and the absence of discomfort. But, as they soak in life's comforts, they also subtly begin to absorb a temporal worldview which ultimately leads to a wasted life and, even worse, to a lost soul if they have never come to know Christ as their Savior.

**But.**

What a significant "but." This little word introduces a perfect contrast and opens the way before us to the second pole, or extreme, of this psalm. This contrast is then detailed and expanded on multiple levels throughout the remaining verses.

| VERSES | THE BLESSED MAN (1:1) | THE PERISHING MAN (1:6) |
|--------|----------------------|-------------------------|
| 1:3-4 | There is a sturdy tree | and there is chaff blown by the wind |
| 1:5-6 | There are the righteous | and there are the wicked |
| 1:1,5 | There are those who do not stand in the way of sinners | and those unable to stand (*or, will lose their case*) in judgment |
| 1:1-2 | There is the law of the Lord | and there is the counsel of the wicked |
| | "**But** *his delight is in the law of the Lord.*" | Contrast. Polarization. How great the disparity! |

Those who would delight in the law of the Lord must be aware that His law flows in direct opposition to the current of this age. Having the law of the Lord as your passion, and holding to the definition that to know God is true prosperity, run contrary to the mindset of the world. You must choose. Now, hang on! Before you conclude, "I've already chosen!" allow some hard questions for introspection: Do I treat God's Word as an option to consider or as a command to obey? In what areas of life do my actions suggest that God's Word is a good idea rather than proclaim it as His divine inspiration?

When the Word of God delineates a clear course of action, intentional partial obedience is actually disobedience. This does not mean that God will never use our partial obedience (or disobedience) for His purposes. His mercy is always at work. **But if we obey God's Word only when we feel like it or only when we fully understand what He is asking, we are treating Jesus Christ as nothing more than a good teacher. It is when we obey Him** *fully***, regardless of our understanding of "Why?" that we genuinely exalt Him as Lord.** This is not a vague concept in Scripture. The Lord tells us in Isaiah 55:8-9, *"For My thoughts are not your thoughts, neither are your ways My ways, declares the Lord. For as the heavens are higher than the earth, so are My ways higher than your ways and My thoughts than your thoughts."*

> **DO I TREAT GOD'S WORD AS AN OPTION TO CONSIDER OR AS A COMMAND TO OBEY?**

**The blessed life is not a life full of rights for self; it is a life of full resignation to the Savior.**

Imagine someone taking up the cross and then declaring, "I have rights, you know." The one bearing a cross is not heading on vacation; he's heading to his own crucifixion. Yet consider the good news. When I resign myself to Christ, I'm resigning myself to, and trusting in, the One who loves me far more than I love myself. I don't have to understand the entire process; I only need to know Him. Remember, Psalm 1:2 says, *"But his delight...."* Don't misunderstand. This is

**I DON'T HAVE TO UNDERSTAND THE ENTIRE PROCESS; I ONLY NEED TO KNOW HIM.**

not a decision to be intentionally polarized from other people or from the world itself. Rather, it is an intentional choice to follow God's law, God's way, in this world—regardless of the repercussions.

**SELF-EXAMINATION:** Are you facing decisions today that seem to polarize you from the expectations of others, the affirmation of loved ones, or approval from the world? Are you focused on the repercussions you may face, or are you fixed on your responsibility to the Word? The blessed man's delight is not a delight that *seeks ease*, but one that *evokes suffering*. **Remind yourself of one thing: This isn't a decision to walk away from the world, but a determination to walk decidedly in the Word.** Polarization is a by-product of association. You don't have to try to be polarized. It will happen naturally as you allow the pursuit of God's law to dictate your delight. Your decision and your delight will soon line up with one another and will merge to unite as one so that when you are asked, "Where is your true delight (based on faith, not feelings)?" your clear response will be:

A TIME FOR

*Reflection*

> *My heart is leaning on the Word, the written Word of God:*
> *Salvation by my Savior's name, salvation through His blood.*
> *I need no other argument, I need no other plea;*
> *It is enough that Jesus died, and that He died for me.*[4]

**QUESTIONS TO CONSIDER:** Before addressing these questions, take a few minutes to write down your initial thoughts and reactions to this chapter. What stands out to you? What questions come to mind? What does your flesh initially want to resist?

1. In what areas of your life are you treating God's Word as a good idea to consider rather than the absolute authority to obey? (Be specific.)

2. What steps of obedience will likely polarize you from the mentality of the world surrounding you?

3. In what areas are you straddling the world's line rather than separating yourself to God's Word?

4. Reflect on the priorities of your daily life/schedule. How do your priorities reveal either polarization from the world or the pull toward it?

5. It was said, *"The blessed life is not a life full of rights for self; it is a life of full resignation to the Savior."* Make a list of "rights" that you think you have. How might your perceived rights distract you from absolute surrender?

6. In times of polarization, the feeling of alienation can be a normal, and sometimes overwhelming, sentiment. What words of Scripture can you use to encourage and motivate yourself and others when feeling ostracized by the world?

7. In what areas (i.e. habits, friends, etc.) of your life are you standing at the summit of a potential slippery slope—even if those areas seem harmless at the moment?

# Notes

# THE *Practice* OF THE BLESSED MAN

**PSALM 1:1-3** *Blessed is the man who walks not in the counsel of the wicked, nor stands in the way of sinners, nor sits in the seat of scoffers; but his delight is in the law of the Lord, and on His law he meditates day and night. He is like a tree planted by streams of water that yields its fruit in its season, and its leaf does not wither. In all that he does, he prospers.*

**BIG IDEA:**

WE **PRACTICE** WHATEVER WE DELIGHT IN. FIND A PERSON'S PRACTICE, AND YOU'LL DISCOVER THEIR DELIGHT.

There is an old proverb dating back at least to the 1500s that says, "Practice makes perfect." New York Times best-selling author Malcolm Gladwell claims that 10,000 hours of deliberate practice are needed to become world-class in any field. But whether or not these proverbs and principles are fully accurate, what one practices and how one practices it will greatly impact one's life.[5]

Take a deeper look into Psalm 1:2—*"But his delight is in the law of the Lord, and on His law he meditates day and night."* There is a specific activity that characterizes, controls, and consumes the blessed man's life; this blessed life didn't just happen to him. And there was a definite decision made. The psalmist tells us clearly, *"On His law he meditates day and night."* We'll save the discussion on how he applied this principle of meditation for the next chapter, but for now, consider his practice.

What is *practice*?

Simply put, practice is "to carry out or perform an activity habitually or regularly." The reality of our lives would suggest that we *do* practice our true delight, our passion. Whether it be sports, work, family, or the pursuit of some goal, dream, or person, **find your practice and you'll discover your** *delight*. Don't forget, this type of delight is not some party-style delight that feels good all the time. Rather, it is an earnest desire and passion which believes that the pursuit of this delight will lead to true prosperity. Why else would business executives put in strenuous hours after quitting time? Why would elite athletes continue to sweat it out in a gym long after others have left? And when they finally do go home, what can you expect to find them doing? Pretty much the same thing: watching YouTube videos, reading articles and books, and conversing with others about what they *practice*—their delight. But it doesn't even stop there. You'll also find that they are likely to invest great financial expenditures on anything which they perceive will help them in their *practice toward prosperity*.

**THE REALITY OF OUR LIVES WOULD SUGGEST THAT WE DO PRACTICE OUR TRUE DELIGHT, OUR PASSION.**

Jesus tells a parable in Matthew 13:44 of a man who demonstrated his passion for his practice. We are told that *"in his joy he goes and sells all that he has and buys that field."* Why would anyone do such a thing? Why would anyone sell *everything* in order to be able to purchase *one* thing? The reason is clear: They have found the treasure they sought. *With joy* the man sells all he has. He cannot liquidate his assets fast enough. The sacrifice can't

**WHY WOULD ANYONE SELL** *EVERYTHING* **IN ORDER TO BE ABLE TO PURCHASE** *ONE THING*? **THE REASON IS CLEAR...**

compare to the reward. Any present discomfort pales in comparison to the treasure that awaits. His eyes are fixed on one thing.

Likewise, our practice will identify our treasure, and, in that, our heart will be exposed. In the words of Jesus Christ, *"For where your treasure is, there your heart will be also"* (Matthew 6:21).

**DO I RESOLUTELY PRACTICE WHAT I *CLAIM* TO DELIGHT IN?**

Perhaps the question we need to ask ourselves is this: Do I resolutely practice what I *claim* to delight in? Pause and ponder the implications of that question. Is the Word of God really your practice? Remember, **our practice reflects our view of true prosperity**. If we value souls, we will engage consistently in the lives of others. If we value compassion, we will reach out sacrificially. If we value comfort, we will seek to accumulate. But if knowing God is our definition of true prosperity, we will be willing to invest whatever it takes to know Him more intimately. *Am I willing?* Paul, an apostle of Christ, said, *"But whatever gain I had, I counted as loss for the sake of Christ"* (Philippians 3:7).

If God's Word is truly your delight, your practice will be to both absorb it and obey it. But we need to be honest about this: **Practice is *not* easy**. It's not natural. It takes hard work, concerted effort. Don't expect to fall in love with the Word merely by asking God to instill in you this passion. You'll need to invest in it. *"Taste and see that the Lord is good"* (Psalm 34:8). Those who seek will find.

If I struggle to enjoy God's Word, or simply don't see much value in it, it's not because God's Word has failed. It's most likely that I have quit the pursuit prematurely. But don't let past disappointment in your own practice of God's Word discourage you. Rather, let it be the catalyst and encouragement to get up and go on. Solomon urges us on with these words: *"Search for it as for hidden treasures"* (Proverbs 2:4). How likely are you to find precious metals on the surface of the earth? No, you'll need a shovel, some sweat, and a willingness to suffer.

**DON'T LET PAST DISAPPOINTMENT IN YOUR OWN PRACTICE OF GOD'S WORD DISCOURAGE YOU.**

Brother Lawrence said in his journals (now published as *The Practice of the Presence of God*), *"Do not be discouraged by the resistance you will encounter from your human nature. You must go against your human inclinations. Often, in the beginning, you will think that you are wasting time, but you must go on. Be determined and persevere in it until death, despite all the difficulties."*[6]

**An instrument is tuned as notes are played and adjusted. A ship is turned as its rudder prompts it to change course. A man is changed by his God as he meditates on the Word day and night.**

**SELF-EXAMINATION:** Perhaps we understand by now that this is not about feelings. Feelings fluctuate. Nor is it merely about *your* faith. Faith may also fluctuate—and even falter, as it did with Christ's disciples. Specifically, this is about the foundation on which your faith rests. Is your faith founded on who God is and on the certainty that what He says is not only true but is also for your ultimate good and His eternal glory? If God is who He says He is, shouldn't you be willing to make His law your delight? Practice is a decision, and it's a declaration. What will you choose to practice today?

A TIME FOR

*Reflection*

> *What will it be like when I see You,*
> *And all of Your glory and power?*
> *Will I hear 'Well done, faithful servant;*
> *You treasured your hours'?*
> *Oh may I be found in Your presence,*
> *Paying no mind to my needs,*
> *Consumed by Your infinite wonder,*
> *Content at Your feet,*
> *I think I'll just linger a little while longer.*[7]

**QUESTIONS TO CONSIDER:** Before addressing these questions, take a few minutes to write down your initial thoughts and reactions to this chapter. What stands out to you? What questions come to mind? What does your flesh initially want to resist?

1. What do you claim to delight in? What would your friends say you delight in?

2. Run a rough tally on your time expenditure. What does it reveal as your true delight? What activity characterizes, controls, and consumes your life?

3. What keeps you from seeing the reward as more valuable than the sacrifice?

4. What do you intentionally practice (make a conscientious effort to carry out or perform) on a day-to-day basis?

5. How does your practice line up with what you claim to delight in? In what specific areas are you aware of the need to train for the constant spiritual warfare around you?

6. At what point have you prematurely stopped in your practice of delighting in God's Word? And, why did you stop (discouragement, busyness, etc.)?

7. Think of the way one might practice an instrument or a sport. What might this level of dedication look like in the practice of delighting in God's Word? (Think through routine, teachers, equipment, etc.).

# Notes

# THE *Possessiveness* OF THE BLESSED MAN

**PSALM 1:1-3** *Blessed is the man who walks not in the counsel of the wicked, nor stands in the way of sinners, nor sits in the seat of scoffers; but his delight is in the law of the Lord, and on His law he **meditates** day and night. He is like a tree planted by streams of water that yields its fruit in its season, and its leaf does not wither. In all that he does, he prospers.*

**BIG IDEA:**

BIBLICAL MEDITATION INVOLVES PROTECTIVE **POSSESSIVENESS**, STANDING OVER AND SLOWLY DEVOURING GOD'S LAW. IF YOU KNOW HOW TO WORRY ABOUT WORLDLY CARES, YOU KNOW HOW TO MEDITATE ON GOD'S WORD.

well on one word: *"Meditates."*

The word in Hebrew is *hagah* and could mean "moan, growl, utter, mutter, devise," or even "plot." Visualizing this word in picture form may help us grasp its impact. In Isaiah 31:4 the word *hagah* is employed: *"As a lion or a young lion growls over his prey...."* There you have it. It's the word *growls*. This is the word the psalmist uses to portray the blessed man's meditation.

But take a closer look. This isn't just any type of growling.

Growing up in Senegal, West Africa, we had two Dachshunds, literally meaning "badger dogs," Taffy and Tina by name. They were fun dogs, full of personality, but when they tracked Gambian pouched rats, sometimes by tunneling underground, their personality changed. As an aside, these rodents (including tail) could measure nearly one meter (over a yard) long. Perhaps this was the creature of Princess Buttercup's concern in *The Princess Bride* when she feared the R.O.U.S. (Rodents of Unusual

Size). Anyway, back to the dogs. Whenever a bloody battle ended with a dead rat, it didn't matter how friendly our dogs *typically* were. They then became protectors of their prey, sitting over it, threatening anyone who would come near (until such time as my dad offered them something better, like a tasty bone or a piece of meat, to lure them away from the rat so he could bury it outside the yard). There you have an illustration of *hagah.*

This word suggests **possessiveness**.

And this is the picture painted for us in Psalm 1:2—*"On His law he meditates day and night."* He growls over it. He protects it. He devours it slowly. Bone by bone. He possesses it.

The psalmist declared, *"I remember You on my bed, I meditate [hagah] on You in the night watches"* (Psalm 63:6 NKJV). What can we learn about meditation from this? Well, first off, we can learn something about what it is *not*. Meditation is *not* the emptying of the mind. To the contrary, it is a filling and a focusing of the mind.

> **MEDITATION IS NOT THE EMPTYING OF THE MIND. TO THE CONTRARY, IT IS A FILLING AND A FOCUSING OF THE MIND.**

Perhaps there is another way to understand this concept of meditation. Think of it in relation to worrying. **If you know how to worry, you know how to meditate.** Same idea. Both are a rehearsing of the same thing over and over. Yet obviously there is a grand difference between the two. Worrying occupies our thoughts with the possibility of a future where God might fail to be fully good. In biblical meditation, we settle our mind on the sure promises of God's Word. We allow His law to take control of every area of our life that isn't yet conformed to the heart of God. Worrying brings restlessness, while biblical meditation brings rest.

**WORRYING BRINGS RESTLESSNESS, WHILE BIBLICAL MEDITATION BRINGS REST.**

Allow one clarification.

When I say "a rehearsing of the Word," I'm not referring to a vain repetition of words but to a thoughtful dwelling upon the text. Repetition in itself is neither a negative nor a positive practice intrinsically. Memorizing and meditating involve much repetition, but repetition for the mere sake of repetition can, in fact, be counterproductive.

The question is not, "Do you meditate?" **Everyone meditates**. Psalm 2:1 tells us that *"the peoples plot in vain."* The word for plot? *Hagah.* They are meditating as well. But on what are the wicked meditating? They are meditating on how to take counsel against the Lord God and His Anointed (Jesus Christ). Our minds collect many thoughts in a day, but *where* do we allow our thoughts to *rest*? That is the question. What do you daydream about? What do you spend great time mulling over, pondering, contemplating, journaling on, or worrying about?

**OUR MINDS COLLECT MANY THOUGHTS IN A DAY, BUT *WHERE* DO WE ALLOW OUR THOUGHTS TO *REST?***

How do we *rest* our thoughts on the Word?
How do we *dwell* on the text?

In 2 Corinthians 10:5, we are reminded to *"take every thought captive to obey Christ."* Take inventory on what we absorb daily. Consider the traffic in our minds—from the myriad of ads to the gigabytes of data to the profusion of people's opinions that we process each day. Do we take it all into captivity by running it through the filter of God's Word? Everything? What if we passed absolutely everything through the filter of meditation on His Word? Wherever you find such a filter, you will find the truly blessed man. Why? He not only prospers, but he sees daily life through eternal eyes.

**SELF-EXAMINATION:** Is your time in the Word rushed? When did you last enjoy time with God without any time constraints? What area of your life isn't being filtered by God's Word? What causes you to worry, to waste time, or to sin in your mind? Meditating on God's Word is the antidote. Meditation isn't about speed; it's about intimacy. A slow devouring. The blessedness of lingering and enjoying the purifying, filling, and satisfying Word of God. May we choose this. May we choose Him.

A TIME FOR

*Reflection*

> May the Word of God dwell richly
> In my heart from hour to hour,
> So that all may see I triumph
> Only through His power.[8]

**QUESTIONS TO CONSIDER: Before addressing these questions, take a few minutes to write down your initial thoughts and reactions to this chapter. What stands out to you? What questions come to mind? What does your flesh initially want to resist?**

1. In what areas of your life do you practice emptying your mind of certain things without also filling it with thoughts of eternal things?

2. Throughout your day, what do you fill your mind with? What do you daydream about? What do you spend great time contemplating, mulling over, pondering, journaling on?

3. In what areas of your life do you mindlessly absorb thoughts without taking them captive (sports, advertisement, media, entertainment, blogs, reviews, etc.)?

4. What do you worry about? What can you learn about meditation from your practice of worrying? Since worry is a sin (remember the definition we discussed), what worry do you need to confess to God? What do your worries reveal about your thoughts of God's character?

5. What thoughts and worries are intensified because you don't filter them through the Word?

6. What might it look like practically if you were to take your moment-by-moment thoughts and run them through the filter of God's Word?

7. Look at your schedule. Find one slot in your week where you can have unhurried, quality time meditating in God's Word. What makes you hesitant to give this time to Him?

# Notes

# THE *Priority* OF THE BLESSED MAN

**PSALM 1:1-3**    *Blessed is the man who walks not in the counsel of the wicked, nor stands in the way of sinners, nor sits in the seat of scoffers; but his delight is in the law of the Lord, and on His law **he meditates day and night**. He is like a tree planted by streams of water that yields its fruit in its season, and its leaf does not wither. In all that he does, he prospers.*

## BIG IDEA:

BY GIVING **PRIORITY** TO GOD'S WORD, WE CALIBRATE OUR DAILY PURSUIT WITH THE ETERNAL BEFORE STEPPING INTO THE TEMPORAL.

*I*n many parts of the world, the preferred configuration at an intersection is a roundabout rather than a traffic signal. I am certainly no traffic authority, but in my opinion, roundabouts seem to be an invitation for chaos. Whichever car has the right-of-way is said to have priority. Everyone else must yield to it. Thus, we find our word.

**Priority**.

The definition of the word *priority* is "the right to take precedence or to proceed before others." This idea emerges clearly in the latter portion of Psalm 1:2—*"on His law he meditates **day and night**."* But one's priority isn't always obvious at first glance. God's Word may occupy a great part of our life, or even be the authority of our life, but that does not guarantee that it is the absolute priority of our life. In the morning when we wake up, do we check out social media before reading the Scriptures? Do we feed our earthly stomach before filling our soul? Do a few minutes of extra sleep take priority over committing the day to our God in humble surrender?

Priority reveals the condition of our heart. This man *"meditates day and night."* Let's not miss the point. This is *not* an obligation to fulfill. This is an opportunity to seize.

**GOD DOESN'T LOVE US ANY LESS IF HE IS NOT OUR PRIORITY IN THE DAY, BUT WE MAY *EXPERIENCE* AND *ENJOY* HIS LOVE LESS.**

God doesn't love us any less if He is not our priority in the day, but we may *experience* and *enjoy* His love less.

When God is pushed from the place of priority, things quickly fall out of order. We need to ask ourselves, "Are we keeping first things first?" Do we invite God to form our day, or do we merely try to fit Him into our day? Now, before excuses fill your mind, understand the underlying principle of the blessed life. This isn't about secondary issues such as whether you're a morning person or a night person. This is about priority. The blessed man gives God both, *"day and night."*

An older friend in Northern Ireland once gave me this advice: *"No Bible, no breakfast. No Bible, no bed."* This is not legalism. It's an invitation. The psalmist exclaimed in Psalm 119:148, *"My eyes are awake before the watches of the night, that I may meditate on Your promise."* And Jesus also had this practice. In Mark 1:35, we read, *"And rising very early in the morning, while it was still dark, He departed and went out to a desolate place, and there He prayed."* What better example to follow?

**GOOD ADVICE: "NO BIBLE, NO BREAKFAST. NO BIBLE, NO BED." THIS IS NOT *LEGALISM*. IT'S AN *INVITATION*.**

There is something beautiful about first *"[setting our] minds on things that are above, not on things that are on earth"* (Colossians 3:2).

**When we calibrate our daily pursuit with the eternal before stepping into the temporal it enables us to see the temporal in the light of the eternal.** The call of Christ is to *"seek first the kingdom of God and His righteousness"* (Matthew 6:33). Seek first—before all else.

Many have better mental clarity later in the day or have responsibilities that start early. I don't discourage using your most alert moments for focused worship and study. But regardless of your most alert time, allow me to strongly encourage you to begin each day by setting your mind on things above. Doing so will set the direction of your perspective and your attitude. There is a vitality which comes to the follower of Christ who gives priority to first running their desires, thoughts, and plans through the filter of God's Word.

[I] STRONGLY ENCOURAGE YOU TO BEGIN EACH DAY BY SETTING YOUR MIND ON THINGS ABOVE. DOING SO WILL SET THE DIRECTION OF YOUR PERSPECTIVE AND YOUR ATTITUDE.

Again, this is *not* about feelings. It's about a heart condition. There will be many days when we will not *feel* like prioritizing God's Word, but our action is a declaration of our need. We must remember who we are and who He is. He is glorified when our flesh is surrendered to His mind and to His ways.

Our *delight* will determine our *priority*.

Consider the following thoughts, not as dogmatic theology, but as encouragement between friends who want to live for Christ. Tithing is mentioned often in churches, but almost always in reference to money. We often hear of giving 10% of our income to the Lord, but let's take it to another level[9] (please take time to read this end note).What if we devoted 10% of our time to quietness before God? Now, before suggesting that we're too busy, remember, it all comes down to an ordering (and reordering) of our life. It is a personal decision. If our priority is a certain salary or position, our entire agenda will revolve around that priority. If our priority is physical health, we will set our schedule for such things as proper exercise and sleep.

**CONSIDER WHAT THE IMPACT ON YOUR LIFE WOULD BE IF YOU WERE TO SET ASIDE 10% OF YOUR MORNING AT THE ONSET OF YOUR DAY TO FOCUS SOLELY ON ETERNAL THINGS.**

According to Nielsen (a North American authority on media usage), in 2019, Americans spent over 11 hours per day interacting with media content.[10] Though I'm not sure how much of that time is focused, undistracted usage, it does add up to nearly half the day. Consider what the impact on your life would be if you were to set aside 10% of your morning at the onset of your day to focus solely on eternal things. That's 144 minutes (2 hours and 24 minutes). **Oh, the filter our minds would have for the day were we to employ such a practice!**

Clearly, prioritizing God's Word will look different for each person.

The young mother who must feed her baby in the night, those caring for their aged parents, the individual working the third shift—each situation is different, but what would your relationships, work, quiet time, and leisure look like if you prioritized God's Word? How would this affect each area of your life? Again, don't read these thoughts as condemnation, but let them be fuel for introspection. Ask yourself, "Is it my priority to allow the Lord to form my day?" This may sound absurd or extreme, but asking this may well reveal that the world's priorities

**ASK YOURSELF, "IS IT MY PRIORITY TO ALLOW THE LORD TO FORM MY DAY?"**

actually claim the prime position in your life. Spending hours watching sports or a movie is a societal norm. Watching a video on Youtube and then sticking around for the next few that play automatically is commonplace. **Imagine if we handled the Word of God with such priority?** Such prioritization is not dependent on circumstances but on the intentionality of the heart. Where is my heart truly set? This is not a formula, and it's not about numbers. It *is* about the heart.

TURN THE PAGE
FOR A TIME OF
*Reflection*

**SELF-EXAMINATION:** Allow a few questions to identify present priorities: With what topic do I usually begin conversations? What do I want to make sure people know about me? What are my priorities in spending money? What part of my schedule do I most quickly protect as sacred? In Psalm 1, the blessed man establishes his priority in the law of the Lord. This is where he chooses to meditate *"day and night."* May our priority be on things eternal, sitting at the feet of Jesus.

A TIME FOR

*Reflection*

*We need to talk. I've missed my time with you.*
*If you could just slow down then maybe I could get through.*
*See, I've made some special plans.*
  *It depends on how you choose.*
*I know you would understand, if I could only talk to you.*
*When was the last time we had a quiet time.*
*It seems you're always making lists*
  *of more important things to do.*
*It's been a long time since we've had our own time.*
*And it breaks my heart to say it, but I've missed you.[11]*

**QUESTIONS TO CONSIDER:** Before addressing these questions, take a few minutes to write down your initial thoughts and reactions to this chapter. What stands out to you? What questions come to mind? What does your flesh initially want to resist?

1. How do you *intentionally* set your heart right before the Lord at the start of a day?

2. What have you placed as your priority above God's Word?

3. What would your relationships, work, quiet time, conversations, and leisure look like if you prioritized God's Word?

4. Do your actions reflect the "heart" you *think* you have? Does your intentionality to spend time alone before God early in the day dictate decisions throughout your day?

5. How would your day look different if you allowed God to form it?

6. What are you not willing to give up in order to prioritize active meditation day and night? Why not?

7. What would an outsider observing your life say is the priority in your life?

# Notes

_____

_____

_____

_____

_____

_____

_____

_____

_____

_____

_____

_____

_____

_____

_____

_____

_____

# THE *Preoccupation* OF THE BLESSED MAN

**PSALM 1:1-3** *Blessed is the man who walks not in the counsel of the wicked, nor stands in the way of sinners, nor sits in the seat of scoffers; but his delight is in the law of the Lord, **and on His law he meditates day and night.** He is like a tree planted by streams of water that yields its fruit in its season, and its leaf does not wither. In all that he does, he prospers.*

**BIG IDEA:**

A PREOCCUPATION WITH GOD'S WORD IS A TAKING CAPTIVE OF EVERY THOUGHT TO OBEY THE MIND OF CHRIST. JESUS DOESN'T WANT TO BE PART OF OUR DAY. HE IS OUR LIFE.

Having examined in Psalm 1:2 the prioritization of God's Word in our life, this next angle may feel like mere repetition, but closer inspection reveals an entirely new dimension. Consider this blessed man who moves from prioritization to...

**Preoccupation.**

There is a phrase I often use in communicating the call of Christ: "Jesus doesn't want to be part of your life. He wants it all." In the light of that truth, let me add, *Jesus doesn't want to be a mere part of your day (even if He is the priority).* He wants it all. If you belong to the Lord Jesus, He is your life, as Colossians 3:3-4 reminds us: *"For you have died, and your life is hidden with Christ in God. When Christ who is your life appears, then you also will appear with Him in glory."* He wants our days plugged into His eternal purpose.

Preoccupation is different from priority. A priority is that which comes first, and it is that which is primary—both necessary positions for the Word of God to fill in our life. But this blessed man doesn't have the Word of God only as his priority; it is also the preoccupation of his life. Consider it like this: **Our time with God is not an event in our day but a constant lifestyle.** Colossians 1:18 declares that our perspective should be *"that in everything He might be preeminent."*

I do not meet with God in the morning (priority), and then walk away thinking, "I've had my time with God for today." Yes, like any good relationship, we need un-broken, non-multitasking, intimate time with the living God. But meditation isn't meant to be efficient; it's intimate. So preoccupation goes beyond that. The individual in Psalm 1 meditates on the law of the Lord *"day and night."* It controls his schedule, his day, his activities.

**MEDITATION ISN'T MEANT TO BE EFFICIENT; IT'S INTIMATE.**

A preoccupation is that which dominates or engrosses the mind to the exclusion of other thoughts. The etymology of *preoccupation* comes from the Latin meaning "to seize beforehand." God literally seizes our heart beforehand, enabling us to see life through the lens of His Word rather than through the lens of the world. In this way, He equips us to respond moment by moment to His Spirit.

Please don't misunderstand this truth.

This is not about deserting your duties, devaluing doing the dishes or changing diapers, or discarding dreams. On the contrary, the law of the Lord dominates the blessed man's conversation, decisions, attitudes, and thoughts *while* he carries out the necessary tasks of each day. **So for us, the Word of God, the law of the Lord, should hijack the way we do everything, the attitude in which we do everything, and the passion with which we do everything.** I use the word *hijack* because there is a battle going on with our flesh. A preoccupation with God's Word is a taking captive of our moments to obey the mind of Christ. Sometimes, asking simple questions can be a catalyst to taking our moments captive: How does this thought, action, or attitude bring honor to God? What does God want to do *in me* through this situation? Am I seeking God's glory or pursuing my own agenda?

> A PREOCCUPATION WITH GOD'S WORD IS A TAKING CAPTIVE OF OUR MOMENTS TO OBEY THE MIND OF CHRIST.

Such daily hijacking brings more meaning to everything *and* puts it in proper perspective. It exalts the value of otherwise menial activities, such as burping a baby, delivering a cup of coffee, or asking a friend about their day. It makes us challenge our motives when pursuing the things the world praises, and it appraises menial tasks, which the world deems insignificant, as being of utmost value in the light of eternity.

In the previous chapter, we discussed the vitality that comes from **first** putting our desires, thoughts, and agenda through the filter of God's Word. Now let's take it a step further. Do we, **moment by moment**, pass the ideas, fashions, trends, opinions, posts, and attitudes of the world through the filter of the law of the Lord? The church in Ephesus was admonished for having *"abandoned the love you had at first"* (Revelation 2:4). **Their problem was one of preeminence rather than of prominence. Christ was prominent among them, but He was no longer the preoccupation of their days.**

The blessed man was preoccupied by the Word of God—it had seized him beforehand. **He was able to see the culture of his day through the eyes of the Word instead of through the eyes of the world. Do I?** C.S. Lewis, in an essay entitled *Is Theology Poetry?* noted, *"I believe in Christianity as I believe that the sun has risen, not only because I see it, but because by it I see everything else."*[12]

A TIME FOR
*Reflection*

**SELF-EXAMINATION:** Are there thoughts throughout your day that you do not pass through the filter of God's Word? As a follower of Christ, are you harboring certain thoughts and refusing to relinquish them to the control of the Holy Spirit? What preoccupies you? When God controls our life, purpose and beauty materialize in every conversation, every hidden attitude, every thought, every action, every plan—since every aspect is now for His eternal glory. *"So, whether you eat or drink, or whatever you do, do all to the glory of God"* (1 Corinthians 10:31). May our lives be preoccupied with the One whose love has captured our heart. As Frances Ridley Havergal concluded in that beautiful hymn:

> *Take my will and make it Thine;*
> *It shall be no longer mine.*
> *Take my heart; it is Thine own.*
> *It shall be Thy royal throne.*
>
> *Take my love, my Lord, I pour*
> *At Thy feet its treasure-store.*
> *Take myself and I will be*
> *Ever, only all for Thee.*[13]

**QUESTIONS TO CONSIDER:** Before addressing these questions, take a few minutes to write down your initial thoughts and reactions to this chapter. What stands out to you? What questions come to mind? What does your flesh initially want to resist?

1. What moments of your day do not commonly pass through the filter of God's Word?

2. How would your day be different and your attitude changed if you allowed God's Word to be the constant filter of your life?

3. What menial tasks have you never looked at through the lens of God's glory? How might your attitude toward these things be different if influenced by meditation on God's Word?

4. What thoughts of man are you refusing to let the Spirit of God in you take captive (assuming you have been born again)?

5. How can you remain preoccupied with God and His Word while going through your day? Any practical disciplines?

6. Are there tasks and activities (that take your time and attention) that you're not doing for the glory of God? Is there a task which you don't see as a vehicle of God's glory? With whom might you discuss this area of your life in order to see more clearly what God wants from it?

7. Since sin is "missing the mark, the bullseye," what areas of preoccupation might you need to confess to God in repentance?

# Notes

## THE *Platform* OF THE BLESSED MAN

**PSALM 1:1-3**   *Blessed is the man who walks not in the counsel of the wicked, nor stands in the way of sinners, nor sits in the seat of scoffers; but his delight is in the law of the Lord, and on His law he meditates day and night. He is like a tree planted by streams of water that yields its fruit in its season, and its leaf does not wither. In all that he does, he prospers.*

**BIG IDEA:**

WHAT WE STAND *FOR* AND WHAT WE STAND *ON* ARE TWO DIFFERENT THINGS. GOD'S WORD IS THE ONLY **PLATFORM** WHICH WILL NEVER COLLAPSE AND IS SURE TO SUPPORT YOU THROUGH EVERY TRIAL OF LIFE.

*I*n our look at the blessed life in Psalm 1 up until now, our focus has been on the inward applications of the practice, priority, and preoccupation of the blessed man. By inward, I'm referring to God's work in the heart of the blessed individual. Now the focus shifts from an inward inspection to an outward recognition as we consider the blessed man's **platform**. Look once more at Psalm 1:2 — *"His delight is in the law of the Lord, and on His law he meditates day and night"*— *on His law*.

The law of the Lord is not only the hub of the blessed man's delight and meditation, but it is also the platform on which he stands. *Platform* has two distinct meanings in English:

(1) A raised surface on which people or things can stand
(2) The declared policy of a party or group

Rather than suggest that it's one or the other for this blessed man, let's go with both.

The use of physical platforms goes back at least to biblical days when Ezra stood on a platform to read the law of the Lord to the people (Nehemiah 8). Sound familiar? This law of the Lord is what the blessed man in Psalm 1 *stands on*. It is also what he *stands up* to proclaim. The Word of God is his *platform*.

Consider your life.

What is your platform? What do you stand on? What is the basis, or foundation, for the claims you make, the goals you pursue, the things you live for? People often say, "I stand *for...*" this or that. Some stand for a political party, some for their sports team, some for their company. Some stand against a certain injustice in society. **And perhaps the things you stand** *for* **are all good and right. But think about this:** *What we stand for* **and** *what we stand on* **are two different things. The one is something** *we* **support; the other supports** *us***.**

Let's be realistic. Anything I stand for or support has the potential to collapse, and probably will at some point. But when I stand on a platform, I am not supporting it; it supports me.

**WHEN I STAND ON A PLATFORM, I AM NOT SUPPORTING *IT*; *IT* SUPPORTS *ME*. I MUST BE VERY CAREFUL TO STAND ONLY ON THOSE THINGS THAT ARE IN COMPLETE SYNC WITH THE WORD OF GOD.**

Because of this, I must be very careful to stand *only* on those things that are in complete sync with the Word of God, the law of the Lord. It is dangerous for me to establish my hope or joy or purpose on anything other than God's Word. If I do, I am only setting myself up for distress, disappointment, and defeat.

Consider the end of your life. Are you standing on anything other than the

Word of God for your salvation and eternal life? It is the Word of God that tells you that Christ loves you, died for you, conquered death for you, and freely offers you the gift of eternal life. My dear friend, if you have not been declared righteous by faith in the finished, perfect, redemptive work of Jesus, your foundation—your platform—will crumble.

In Psalm 1, we find a solid footing on which to stand, but we also learn of foundations that fail. Did you notice in Psalm 1:1 that the one who is perishing (v. 6) *"stands in the way of sinners"*? And verse 5 tells us that *"the wicked will not stand in the judgment."* In other words, those who live apart from the Word of God will not survive the judgment of God. Why not? We will be judged by the law of the Lord (John 12:48), so the only way that we can stand in the final judgment is to have a foundation established on God's perfect law: *"For no one can lay a foundation other than that which is laid, which is Jesus Christ"* (1 Corinthians 3:11).

Will you stand on that final day? I'm speaking *positionally*: are you in Christ? Is Christ your righteousness? And for those who are believers in Christ Jesus, what about *practically*? Will the things you stand for *now* matter on that day when you stand before the Lord Jesus?

> **WILL THE THINGS YOU STAND FOR *NOW* MATTER ON THAT DAY WHEN YOU STAND BEFORE THE LORD JESUS?**

On a personal level, allow a few simple questions. Does your joy fluctuate when things in society, like sports, politics, or news events, rock your life? Is your peace eroded when your plans crash or your dreams fail? Is your hope swayed by election results, a friend's approval, or the outcome of an application? Certainly, there is a place for sadness and mourning, and sometimes we need time to process a loss. But if our attitude, joy, and testimony are determined by earthly circumstances, it could be an indication that we are standing on the world's platform rather than basing our delight, passion, and hope on the law of the Lord.

The primary command given in Scripture to followers of Christ as we engage in spiritual battle is *not* to carry out great exploits; it is to **stand**. Ephesians 6:11, 13 and 14 tell us to *"stand."* Verse 13 also tells us to *"withstand."* The chapter then describes the platform on which we can stand firm against the enemy, which is also the platform from which we can declare the gospel and glory of our God.

And *where* do we stand, according to God's Word?

- We stand in **the gospel** (1 Corinthians 15:1).
- We stand in **grace** (Romans 5:2).
- We stand in **the faith** (1 Corinthians 16:13; 2 Corinthians 1:24).
- We stand in **freedom** from a yoke of slavery to the constraints of the law (Galatians 5:1).
- We stand in **unity**, "one spirit, one mind" in Jesus (Philippians 1:27).
- We stand in **all the will of God** (Colossians 4:12).
- We stand in **the Lord** (Philippians 4:1).

A healthy faith will mourn the brokenness which surrounds us, but if our faith is *shaken* by this ever-changing world, we may have a serious problem. The good news is that we have been offered a foundation which never changes—God's Word: *"Heaven and earth will pass away, but My words will not pass away"* (Matthew 24:35). Where are you standing today?

**SELF-EXAMINATION:** We have seen the implications of this platform positionally and practically, but what about publicly? Do your friends hear more from you about your sports team than about your Savior? Is your schedule taken up more with personal pursuits than it is with God's kingdom and glory? Are you more vocal about a social issue (even a major issue that needs to be addressed) than you are about the one thing (the gospel) that will save people from eternal separation from God and bring them into an intimate relationship with their Creator-Redeemer? Do you focus more on learning the platform of your political party, so you can defend it, than you do on learning the law of the Lord, the heart of God, so you can live it? Jesus said, "You are the light of the world. A city set on a hill cannot be hidden" (Matthew 5:14). May no soul around you or me have any confusion concerning the platform on which we stand.

A TIME FOR

*Reflection*

> *Standing on the promises that cannot fail,*
> *When the howling storms of doubt and fear assail,*
> *By the living Word of God, I shall prevail,*
> *Standing on the promises of God.*[14]

**QUESTIONS TO CONSIDER:** Before addressing these questions, take a few minutes to write down your initial thoughts and reactions to this chapter. What stands out to you? What questions come to mind? What does your flesh initially want to resist?

1. What shakes your confidence and induces anxiety in your life? What is the last thing that really rattled you? What foundation did that reveal?

2. What, if removed, might make you lose desire to carry on or even to live?

3. How do you remind yourself daily of your true foundation and the reason for true peace?

4. Based on the topics of your conversations, what might your friends say you stand for? Would they say you have an equal passion for the soul-saving gospel of Jesus Christ?

5. How might you practically stand more firmly in the things in which God's Word tells us to stand?

6. Do you declare your platform with love? How so?

7. Do you declare your platform primarily with your lips or with your life, or both? Explain. How can the two work together in a complementary way?

# Notes

## THE *Precepts* OF THE BLESSED MAN

**PSALM 1:1-3**   *Blessed is the man who walks not in the counsel of the wicked, nor stands in the way of sinners, nor sits in the seat of scoffers; but his delight is in the law of the Lord, and on His law he meditates day and night. He is like a tree planted by streams of water that yields its fruit in its season, and its leaf does not wither. In all that he does, he prospers.*

**BIG IDEA:**

GOD'S **PRECEPTS** PROVIDE AN OPPORTUNITY FOR US TO PLEASE HIM; THEY ARE A LOVE LETTER CALLING US TO RESPOND TO HIS HEART.

Typically, the word we are about to discuss rarely arouses enthusiasm or excitement, but nothing about this chapter is typical. Our word is *precepts*.

Notice the precepts of this blessed man in Psalm 1:2—*"But his delight is in the law of the Lord."* God's Word is often referred to as His precepts as, for example, in Psalm 119, where this word is used 21 times in the ESV. The simple definition of a precept is "a general rule intended to regulate behavior or thought." But the precepts of the Lord are, literally, the pathway to life: *"I will never forget Your precepts, for by them You have given me life"* (Psalm 119:93).

We do not typically think of the majority of rules and laws as limitations, and certainly not as bondage. Most citizens do not take issue with such laws as "Do not steal another's private property." But consider what the psalmist is saying. It's fascinating! Rarely are laws the source of anyone's *delight!* Be honest. How often do you delight in the speed limit? Or when did you last celebrate the rules and regulations of anything?

This is a truth we need to grab hold of for its eternal value: **If we obey God's laws simply to avoid punishment, we will find little delight in them. BUT His precepts are so much more than that! They are actually an opportunity to please Him and are the pathway to true intimacy with Him.**

The word used for *law* is *torah*. In Psalm 119:18 the worshiper appeals to the Lord, *"Open my eyes, that I may behold wondrous things out of Your law."* In verse 70, he declares, *"I delight in Your law,"* and then he goes on to affirm this same claim in verses 77, 113, 163, and 174. In verse 72, he asserts, *"The law from Your mouth is better to me than thousands of gold and silver pieces."* And in verse 97, *"O how I love Your law! It is my meditation all the day."* Honestly, does this describe you? Or me?

So, what are we missing?

Let's use the aforementioned law of speed limits to help us understand the heart of the blessed man. Recently, God convicted me in this regard. I was typically obeying speed limits because, according to Romans 13:1, I am to *"be subject to the governing authorities."* But I was missing the bottom line. My obedience to the speed limit is not meant to be driven by my fear of judgment; rather, it ought to be an evidence of my desire for fellowship with Jesus Christ. In the same way, **God did not give His precepts to limit my joy, but to reveal His love.** Christ told His disciples, *"Whoever has My commandments and keeps them, he it is who loves Me. And he who loves Me will be loved by My Father, and I will love him and manifest Myself to him"* (John 14:21). God's laws are an open door for us to

**GOD DID NOT GIVE HIS PRECEPTS TO LIMIT MY JOY, BUT TO REVEAL HIS LOVE.**

show our love to Him, just as in them He demonstrates His love for us. **God's precepts are not** *merely* **for our good; they are also an opportunity for us to express our love toward Him.** And how closely knit this opportunity is to the greatest commandment: *"You shall love the Lord your God with all your heart and with all your soul and with all your mind"* (Matthew 22:37).

**IF GOD'S PRECEPTS WERE MERELY ABOUT OUR UPHOLDING JUSTICE, WE WOULD BE DESTROYED. INSTEAD, GOD'S LAW IS A LOVE LETTER CALLING US TO RESPOND TO HIS HEART.**

If God's precepts were merely about our upholding justice, we would be destroyed. Instead, what do we find? God's law is a love letter calling us to respond to His heart. His precepts provide an opportunity for us to declare our passion for our majestic Creator. Even when we were dead in our sins and trespasses—*against God's holy law*—He sent us Jesus Christ and opened the way for us to be made alive in Him (Ephesians 2:1; Colossians 2:13). And so our love for God is founded solely upon His love for us. *"We love because He first loved us"* (1 John 4:19). God invites us not to a religion about Him but into a relationship with Himself. In the words of Timothy Keller, "Religion operates on the principle of 'I obey—therefore I am accepted by God.' The basic operating principle of the gospel is 'I am accepted by God through the work of Jesus Christ—therefore I obey.'" [15]

**RELIGION : "I OBEY—THEREFORE I AM ACCEPTED BY GOD." THE GOSPEL: "I AM ACCEPTED BY GOD THROUGH THE WORK OF JESUS CHRIST—THEREFORE I OBEY." (T. KELLER)**

Returning to our illustration of speed limits, I can say that my perspective has changed. Now when I get into the car, I no longer observe the speed limit for fear of flashing police lights behind me.

Rather, I see it as an opportunity to declare my love for the Lord *since* He told me to *"be subject to the governing authorities."* Perhaps you find this extreme or legalistic. That's okay, but please don't miss the point. God doesn't ask us to understand the "why" behind all His precepts. He simply wants us to trust His character even when we don't understand His reasons.

When we understand God's heart of love, obeying His precepts becomes a splendid opportunity to respond to His heart. In the Garden of Eden, God put one restriction on Adam: to not eat of the tree of the knowledge of good and evil. Why? God didn't restrict Adam in order to bring him trouble or pain—not at all. Rather, the Lord God was giving him a daily opportunity to express his love toward His Creator through obedience. The motivation, the purpose, and the goal of the restriction—it was all about a love *relationship*.

**[GOD] SIMPLY WANTS US TO TRUST HIS CHARACTER EVEN WHEN WE DON'T UNDERSTAND HIS REASONS.**

Love requires choice, not compulsion. Yet, even in our rebellion, God's love proved deeper still. Disobedience to God's law brought consequences to all mankind, *"but where sin increased, grace abounded all the more"* (Romans 5:20), and Christ came and died on the cross to redeem us.

The practical implications of obeying His precepts are thrilling!

Every day is full of *seemingly* small opportunities to declare our love for the Lord simply by walking in His precepts and obeying the words of His mouth. As I choose to follow His precepts, every thought I think, every word I say, and every action I take has the phenomenal potential to be an "I love you, Lord." This is not the burdened life. This is *the blessed life*. No wonder the psalmist couldn't stop speaking of the precious gift of God's law!

**SELF-EXAMINATION:** In what areas do you view God as a forceful master rather than a loving Father? Where are you questioning His precepts rather than delighting in His desire? What do you currently view as a restriction that He wants you to see as an invitation to demonstrate your love for Him?

**Every day we have opportunities to declare our love for the One who will always love us more than we could ever love ourselves. May His precepts be our joy!**

A TIME FOR

*Reflection*

*How long beneath the law I lay in bondage and distress;*
*I toiled the precepts to obey, but toiled without success.*
*Then, to abstain from outward sin*
*was more than I could do;*
*Now, if I feel its power within, I feel I hate it too.*
*Then all my servile works were done*
*a righteousness to raise;*
*Now, freely chosen in the Son, I freely choose His ways.*
*To see the law by Christ fulfilled*
*and hear His pardoning voice,*
*Changes a slave into a child, and duty into choice.*[16]

**QUESTIONS TO CONSIDER:** Before addressing these questions, take a few minutes to write down your initial thoughts and reactions to this chapter. What stands out to you? What questions come to mind? What does your flesh initially want to resist?

1. Before reading this chapter, how did you describe (not define) the term "God's law"? Does your description sound much like the writer of Psalm 119?

2. In what areas of life do God's precepts (commands) seem like a burden?

3. Why do you think you view some of God's precepts as a burden? In what ways might they actually be an opportunity?

4. What seemingly small acts of obedience each day could be opportunities to say, "I love you, Lord!"

5. Describe a time in your life when you delighted in God's precepts.

6. How does your view of God's precepts impact your view of God's heart?

7. Give some examples, real or hypothetical, of how God's precepts are for your good and His glory?

# Notes

# THE *Purity* OF THE BLESSED MAN

**PSALM 1:1-3**   *Blessed is the man who walks not in the counsel of the wicked, nor stands in the way of sinners, nor sits in the seat of scoffers; but his delight is in the law of the Lord, and on His law he meditates day and night. He is like a tree planted by streams of water that yields its fruit in its season, and its leaf does not wither. In all that he does, he prospers.*

**BIG IDEA:**

TO LIVE A LIFE OF **PURITY**, WE MUST FILTER ALL THE INFORMATION, IDEAS, AND INVITATIONS OF THE WORLD THROUGH THE PURE WORD OF GOD.

Sometimes it's the words that *aren't* there that catch one's attention. In this passage, it's what isn't in Psalm 1:2 that stands out. Confusing? Allow me to explain. *"His delight is in the law of the Lord, and on His law he meditates day and night."*

That's it.
There is *nothing* more.

It's not like the blessed man is delighting in books in general, or in academics, philosophy, sports, *and* the law of God. This is a man with a singular focus, a solitary foundation, and a sole fervor. So today we will focus on this blessed man and his **purity**.

*Purity* is simply "the freedom from contamination".

On a trip into the jungles of Peru via an Amazon River tributary, I needed clean water to drink, so I took with me an ultraviolet water-purifying bottle. I could literally grab water out of the

Huallaga River, shake it for 60 seconds under this UV light, and drink the water safely. But imagine for a moment that the water bottle company had intentionally sold me a defective product that would let some bacteria through.

Consider it now through different imagery.

What if someone with a deadly allergy to peanuts suggested that only one peanut be placed in their ice cream? Or a bank executive suggested that the password to his personal financial accounts be shared with only one random individual. We all understand and agree that that would be absurd. We value purity—absolute purity. These examples may seem almost foolish, but isn't this precisely our mentality concerning our spiritual life? In the light of eternity and God's holiness, how can we ever hope to justify such compromise?

**IN THE LIGHT OF ETERNITY AND GOD'S HOLINESS, HOW CAN WE EVER HOPE TO JUSTIFY SUCH COMPROMISE?**

We carefully protect the simple things of life such as health, money, and privacy and wouldn't risk contaminating them. But are we just as careful to guard our soul from contamination, or do we act as though it doesn't matter? Do we care about spiritual purity? What a loud declaration this is that we have adopted the Laodicean lifestyle! We want to be friends simultaneously with the world and with God although God clearly tells us, *"Because you are lukewarm, and neither hot nor cold, I will spit you out of My mouth"* (Revelation 3:16). James, a brother of Jesus, stated, *"Whoever wishes to be a friend of the world makes himself an enemy of God"* (James 4:4). John, a disciple

**WE CAREFULLY PROTECT THE SIMPLE THINGS OF LIFE. DO WE CARE ABOUT SPIRITUAL PURITY?**

who walked with Christ throughout His earthly ministry, reiterated, *"Do not love the world or the things in the world. If anyone loves the world, the love of the Father is not in him"* (1 John 2:15).

**Have we been so blinded spiritually that we not only *accommodate* contamination but actually *invite* it into our lives?** Do not misinterpret this. This is *not* an appeal to avoid the world. This is *not* a warning to not associate with the lost. This is *not* a justification for being awkwardly ignorant of what is happening around you. This *is* an exhortation to process and evaluate, in the light of God's law and love, the things that we absorb each day.

> **THIS IS *NOT* AN APPEAL TO AVOID THE WORLD. THIS IS AN EXHORTATION TO PROCESS AND EVALUATE, IN THE LIGHT OF GOD'S LAW AND LOVE, THE THINGS THAT WE ABSORB EACH DAY**

In Psalm 1:1 the writer begins with *"Blessed is the man who walks not in the counsel of the wicked."* He doesn't say, Blessed is the man who doesn't *hear* the counsel of the wicked. You will hear it everywhere. Counsel in this verse means, "your faculty of forming plans." Turn on the radio or television, open an app on your device, listen to a friend, read a review, or just tune in to your own thoughts, and you'll get the mind and opinion of others. But perhaps you feel defensive and are thinking, "It says, *'counsel of the wicked.'* I'm not wicked. My friends aren't wicked."

Take a deeper look at what the psalmist is saying.

The word used for *wicked* is *rasha,* which simply means "unrighteous." Consider the Greek translation of this word in the Septuagint, *asebes.*

**THE WORD *ASEBES* IS MADE UP OF TWO PARTS:**

| (1) *sébomai* means "to worship or venerate" | (2) the prefix *a-* makes the word *negative* |
| --- | --- |

Putting these pieces together, we see this word *wicked* from another angle:

**"those without worship"**

It describes one who expresses a lack of interest in the things of God, one whose behavior and lifestyle are characterized by an *irreverent attitude*.

What is an irreverent attitude? **An irreverent attitude is one that regards the precepts of God with a mindset of suggestion rather than with a heart of surrender**. Any attitude that doesn't worship God as supreme and place His Word as the absolute authority in all matters of life is irreverent. You understand! And so do I. This attitude-problem affects each of us to varying degrees.

Romans 3:10-12 informs us that we are all unrighteous. *"None is righteous, no, not one; no one understands; no one seeks for God. All have turned aside; together they have become worthless; no one does good, not even one."* We need conversion. We need salvation. We need the Lord Jesus. But after receiving His salvation from our sin, we need His guidance too—pure, uncontaminated guidance which comes through *"the law of the Lord."* In the words of David, *"The words of the Lord are pure words, like silver refined in a furnace on the ground, purified seven times"* (Psalm 12:6).

We need purity to process the information, ideas, and invitations of the world. It's not all bad. The water from the Peruvian river wasn't all bad. That's why I could drink it. It just needed to be filtered so the good of it could be enjoyed. **All of the water needed to be filtered, but not all of it needed to be eliminated.** Most of the time, I couldn't even see what was bad in it. Sure, I could identify the leaves, bugs, and branch fragments that got caught in the initial filter, but the deadly bacteria was hidden. So it is with the thoughts and intents of the heart of the wicked.

Be aware! Contaminants can easily infiltrate our life through channels we deem "safe." We need to imitate the Berean believers in Acts 17:11 who put even the verbal teachings of Paul the apostle through the filter of God's law: *"They received the word with all eagerness, examining the Scriptures daily to see if these things were so."*

**CONTAMINANTS CAN EASILY INFILTRATE OUR LIFE THROUGH CHANNELS WE DEEM "SAFE." IF YOU WANT TO LIVE A PURE LIFE, YOU MUST RUN EVERYTHING THROUGH THE FILTER OF GOD'S WORD.**

This blessed man of Psalm 1 teaches us a profound lesson. If you want to live a pure life, you must run everything through the filter of God's Word, the essential ultimate filter for all decision-making and for living a life of purity. How richly blessed we are to have the gift of God's Word!

TURN THE PAGE
FOR A TIME OF
*Reflection*

**SELF-EXAMINATION:** What decisions do you never run through the filter of God's Word? Dwell on that question. What decisions do you never consult God on? What is your "faculty of forming plans" (counsel) if it isn't God? Just a little unfiltered water, just one peanut, just one random person with my passwords—these are enough to destroy a physical life. Am I as concerned about my spiritual health as I am about my physical health? We need to take our lives seriously and live in the purity that comes only when we pass everything through the filter of God's mind, as revealed in His Scriptures, through the conviction of His Spirit.

A TIME FOR

*Reflection*

> More purity give me, more strength to overcome;
> More freedom from earth-stains, more longing for home;
> More fit for the kingdom, more used I would be,
> More blessed and holy, more, Savior, like Thee.[17]

**QUESTIONS TO CONSIDER:** Before addressing these questions, take a few minutes to write down your initial thoughts and reactions to this chapter. What stands out to you? What questions come to mind? What does your flesh initially want to resist?

1. What contamination do you intentionally allow into your life? Why do you invite this contamination to enter in? How do these (perceived) benefits compare to intimacy with the Lord?

2. Who are the people and what are the things that most influence your thinking and decision-making?

3. What practical effects has *lack* of purity had in your spiritual life? Pray over this question, and leave space for the Holy Spirit to communicate His answer.

4. Looking back over the past year, what decisions have you made to intentionally filter what comes into your life?

5. There are many obvious aspects of life that you know need to be filtered, but what areas of life do you assume don't need a filter (certain friends, Bible studies, family, etc.)? How might this assumption be dangerous?

6. Consider the steps you take to maintain your physical health, to protect yourself from viruses, and to treat any diagnosed infirmity. Now take a few minutes to journal what the same level of intentionality toward holiness would look like for your spiritual health.

7. What practical steps can you take to apply the filter of God's Word moment by moment throughout your day?

# Notes

# THE *Powerlessness* OF THE BLESSED MAN

**PSALM 1:1-3** *Blessed is the man who walks not in the counsel of the wicked, nor stands in the way of sinners, nor sits in the seat of scoffers; but his delight is in the law of the Lord, and on His law he meditates day and night. He is **like a tree** planted by streams of water that yields its fruit in its season, and its leaf does not wither. In all that he does, he prospers.*

**BIG IDEA:**

WE ARE TOTALLY **POWERLESS**, IN OUR OWN EFFORTS, TO LIVE THE VICTORIOUS CHRISTIAN LIFE; WE ARE COMPLETELY DEPENDENT ON GOD, OUR ONLY SOURCE OF LIFE AND STRENGTH.

As we shift our attention forward to Psalm 1:3, a picture emerges that has far-reaching practical implications for everyday life. Our word for this chapter isn't *picture*, but this picture is the framework for the next few distinctives of the blessed man. Notice the simile: *"He is like a tree." Like* indicates that two different things are being compared. Here, the blessed man who meditates day and night on God's Word is being compared to a tree planted by streams of water. We can glean many lessons from this, but for now, let's focus our attention on the **powerlessness** of a tree.

What do we mean?

A tree can certainly demonstrate awesome endurance through storms. And it shows its strength as it extracts water from the ground and sends its sap to every branch, twig, and leaf, supplying their needed nutrients. But that's not our current focus. Take note: God didn't compare us to bedrock; He under-

GOD DIDN'T COMPARE
US TO BEDROCK;
HE UNDERSCORED
THAT WE ARE
LIVING ORGANISMS
WHICH REQUIRE
OUTSIDE SOURCES IN
ORDER TO SURVIVE
AND THRIVE.

scored that we are living organisms which require outside sources in order to survive and thrive.

God gave us the example of a tree which, though beautiful and useful, desperately needs external sustenance. You may have the highest quality seed of the strongest, most beautiful, and most fruitful tree in the world, but, without proper soil, water, and sunshine, that seed will never grow to be a fruitful tree; it will never thrive or produce anything of value. Even if there is some growth initially, it will eventually succumb to its hostile environment and will wither and die.

A tree is utterly dependent, it has an absolute need, and it is evidently powerless to produce fruit without specific resources which exist only outside of itself. And so in this picture we see the blessed man. If we are to thrive in the blessedness that God has designed, we must first acknowledge that it will *not* happen by trying harder but only by surrendering to the control of His Holy Spirit.

A TREE IS UTTERLY
DEPENDENT, IT HAS
AN ABSOLUTE NEED,
AND IT IS EVIDENTLY
POWERLESS TO
PRODUCE FRUIT
WITHOUT SPECIFIC
RESOURCES WHICH
EXIST ONLY OUTSIDE OF
ITSELF [JUST LIKE]
THE BLESSED MAN.

Let's explore this idea by considering a situation.

Ask a few believers who have come to the cross for salvation, "How were you saved?" Though the answers will vary in expression, they will all have the common storyline of a helpless sinner turning from his or her own efforts to the grace of God found in the finished, redemptive work of Jesus Christ. But if you were to ask some believers how to grow in Jesus Christ, you may receive a plethora of responses which would likely add to your confusion.

Perhaps this is because we so easily fall into the Galatians 3:3 trap. Paul asked the local church in Galatia, *"Are you so foolish? Having begun by the Spirit, are you now being perfected by the flesh?"* We each need to ask ourselves, Do I rely on my own strength for growth in Christ and to glorify Him? Or is my habit to lay hold on the only competent and worthy Power beyond myself, the Spirit of God? The fact is, we have no strength, and even no life, apart from Him. In the words of Romans 7:18, *"For I know that nothing good dwells in me, that is, in my flesh. For I have the desire to do what is right, but not the ability to carry it out."* This is the same declaration David made when he said to the Lord, *"You are my Lord; I have no good apart from You"* (Psalm 16:2).

> **DO I RELY ON MY OWN STRENGTH, OR IS MY HABIT TO LAY HOLD ON THE ONLY COMPETENT AND WORTHY POWER BEYOND MYSELF, THE SPIRIT OF GOD?**

Yet on the flip side we find a marvelous truth for all who have placed their faith in Jesus Christ:

> *"You, however, are not in the flesh but in the Spirit, if in fact the Spirit of God dwells in you. Anyone who does not have the Spirit of Christ does not belong to Him.... If the Spirit of Him who raised Jesus from the dead dwells in you, He who raised Christ Jesus from the dead will also give life to your mortal bodies through His Spirit who dwells in you"* (Romans 8:9,11).

Get this: The same Spirit that raised Christ from the dead lives in us! If that truth doesn't ignite my enthusiasm, I am either lost or seriously distracted by this world. The power required to live the victorious Christian life does not grow from my own determination and effort; it comes *"by faith in the Son of God, who loved me and gave Himself for me"* (Galatians 2:20).

There is, however, a danger in this discussion of powerlessness.

One can easily succumb to the lie of worthlessness. This is a tragic misunderstanding. As we reflect on other features of this blessed man, we will find that his powerlessness is *by no means* a gauge of his value, for God's valuation of a soul is not based on man's estimation. You do not need to look any further than the cross of Jesus Christ to understand how much your life is worth to God. And yet, though the blessed man is powerless in himself, his impotence is never an excuse for laziness or carelessness. Instead, it is a call to *dependency*.

> **Ultimately, this is a journey that must end in complete *surrender*.**

**For the tree**, surrender means absorbing the sun, the soil, and the water. **For us**, surrender means absorbing the pure Word, setting up our tent in the presence of God, and trekking our way through life by the Spirit's compass-guidance, being ever careful to not be drawn off course by earthly enticements. (In later chapters, we will dive more deeply into the implications of God's strength and provision for us.)

Recently, someone asked me, "In your opinion, what is one of the primary reasons for the rebellion against God that we see in our culture today?" Though I cannot claim that my answer was well thought-out or even particularly wise, I answered, "Independence." I'm not referring to our independence as a nation but to our independence as individuals. Most specifically, I'm referring to our independence as followers of Christ. **The problem is not that we cry out to God in desperation; rather, it is that we fail to recognize and acknowledge our desperate need of Him and our absolute dependence on Him.**

> SOMEONE ASKED ME, "IN YOUR OPINION, WHAT IS ONE OF THE PRIMARY REASONS FOR THE REBELLION AGAINST GOD THAT WE SEE IN OUR CULTURE TODAY?" I ANSWERED, "INDEPENDENCE."

Every human being is innately powerless, and yet, in recognizing our powerlessness, every person who has Christ has an innate strength to be discovered, for the Lord Himself has promised us, *"My grace is sufficient for you, for My power is made perfect in weakness"* (2 Corinthians 12:9)—like a tree, full of potential, yet utterly powerless without The Source of power. May our lives show our utter dependence on His Spirit so that His power might be realized in us and proclaimed through us.

TURN THE PAGE FOR A TIME OF *Reflection*

**SELF-EXAMINATION:** Do we try to be self-sufficient rather than being surrendered to Christ? Do we believe that we are entitled to certain things, or are we just thankful for absolutely everything? Do we see blessings as a recompense for our goodness or as a reception of His grace? Do we deem our reputation as something to reinforce rather than something to relinquish for the sake of His glory?

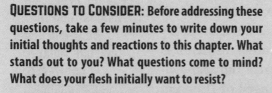

*I need Thee, oh I need Thee, every hour I need Thee!
Oh, bless me now, my Savior—I come to Thee.*[18]

**A TIME FOR**

*Reflection*

**QUESTIONS TO CONSIDER: Before addressing these questions, take a few minutes to write down your initial thoughts and reactions to this chapter. What stands out to you? What questions come to mind? What does your flesh initially want to resist?**

1. Diagnosing the difference between surrendering to God's power and doing things in your own power is, at times, tough to do. What symptoms might you identify in your life that indicate a lack of reliance on God for moment-by-moment strength?

2. How would you describe your decision-making process? Is it built on what you can do in your own strength or on what God can do through you?

3. In what areas of your life are you relying on your own strength?

4. Why is self-reliance our default mode ? Is it because of a lack of trust in God? Is it due to some habitual sin that breaks our fellowship with Him? Take a few moments to identify the root of this problem in your own life (if and when it occurs).

5. A tree needs outside resources to grow (sun, soil, water, etc.). Make a list of things supplied by God on which you are completely dependent for daily survival. (You can start with oxygen, gravity...) Name at least 20.

6. Does recognizing your own powerlessness bring anxiety or joyful trust? Why do you think this is?

7. During good times, we often forget our desperate need for God more than we do in the difficult times. When have you seen this to be the case? (If you need help, just ask yourself what you are not praying about at the present.) Why might this self-sufficiency be your norm?

# Notes

# THE *Plan* OF THE BLESSED MAN

**PSALM 1:1-3** *Blessed is the man who walks not in the counsel of the wicked, nor stands in the way of sinners, nor sits in the seat of scoffers; but his delight is in the law of the Lord, and on His law he meditates day and night. He is **like a tree planted** by streams of water that yields its fruit in its season, and its leaf does not wither. In all that he does, he prospers.*

**BIG IDEA:**

GOD HAS PLANTED US ACCORDING TO HIS **PLAN** SO THAT WE CAN FLOURISH IN THE PURPOSE HE INTENDS FOR US.

What intentionality we find in the simile presented to us in Psalm 1:3. Look again at the phrase which launches this verse: *"He is like a tree planted."* Planted. This tree was not thrown haphazardly to the ground, it did not begin to grow on its own, unnoticed, nor was it later abandoned.

Rather, this tree was deliberately planted for the purpose of growth. Here is *intentionality*. Here we find the gentle hand of a caretaker. Here is a **plan**.

**THIS TREE WAS NOT THROWN HAPHAZARDLY TO THE GROUND. RATHER, THIS TREE WAS DELIBERATELY PLANTED FOR THE PURPOSE OF GROWTH. HERE IS *INTENTIONALITY*.**

Meditate on the verb *plant*. It means "to place or fix in a specified position," and embedded in this word is the word *plan*. Walk through a beautiful garden, and you won't see plants aimlessly placed. You won't normally find a rosebush in the middle of a lawn nor a tree planted right up against the foundation of a house. The placement of each plant is thoroughly considered, strategically assessed, and carefully planned.

If you were to visit the gardens at the Palace of Versailles in France, you might observe that every Corsican Pine, Beech, Poplar, Chestnut, and Hawthorn tree has been strategically planted. If we expect such planning and intentionality from a human mind, how much more should we expect it from the mind of the omniscient God! *"Like a tree planted by streams of water."* Placed. Fixed. An integral part of a greater arrangement. Your existence is not an accident, nor are your circumstances.

**YOUR EXISTENCE IS NOT AN ACCIDENT, NOR ARE YOUR CIRCUMSTANCES.**

And where is the Gardener's choice place for our planting? It is by the stream of His Word. But are we resisting this environment designed for our growth? Are we rejecting His placement of us and His plan for our lives? Are we reacting to our surroundings rather than responding to our loving Lord who longs for us to thrive?

God plants us tactically where we can more than merely survive. **He plants us with a plan in place and places us within His plan.** He puts us where we can flourish in the purpose He intends for us: the purpose of knowing Him and of being sanctified and conformed to the likeness of Jesus Christ.

**HE PLANTS US WHERE WE CAN FLOURISH IN THE PURPOSE HE INTENDS FOR US.**

The truth of Psalm 1 is expressed in Philippians 1:6—*"And I am sure of this, that He who began a good work in you will bring it to completion at the day of Jesus Christ."* We must not misunderstand the Almighty's plan and intention. **God is not *our* life coach to help *us* reach *our* goals. He is Lord—and He wants us to thrive in *His* plan for our lives and, in the process, to get to know Him intimately.**

One of the most misapplied verses in Scripture is Jeremiah 29:11. Speaking to the Jews in Babylonian exile, God reminds them, *"For I know the plans I have for you, declares the Lord, plans for welfare and not for evil, to give you a future and a hope."* Yet we twist this verse and cling to it as though it were a promise that "God wants me to have a great life." Sure He does, but only within the context of His plans. Look at the verse before this (that would be Jeremiah 29:10). In my words (check it out yourself), *"You're going to be dragged into exile for seventy years. Most of you are never coming home again* [the returning remnant is spoken of elsewhere]. *But I know the plans that I have for you."* In other words, God's plans are way bigger than our mere earthly existence.

This isn't merely about "your story." In fact, this really isn't even about your story. This is about *His* story. *History.* This is about *His glory.* And this is great news! Why? It means that cancer isn't the problem. Your career isn't the issue. Your community isn't the obstacle. Your circumstances are not the concern. You are loved. In Christ, you are redeemed. In Him, you have been planted. You are sealed. You have a purpose—His purpose. You are part of a plan—*His* plan.

**IN CHRIST, YOU ARE REDEEMED. IN HIM, YOU HAVE BEEN PLANTED. YOU ARE PART OF A PLAN — *HIS* PLAN.**

TURN THE PAGE FOR A TIME OF *Reflection*

**SELF-EXAMINATION:** Are you unhappy with the place in which God has planted you? Are you questioning the Gardener's plan? Have you been inviting God into your plans instead of investing your life in God's plan? "Like a tree planted." Take a few minutes to think on these questions. Do you know God's plan for your life? If you do, are you pushing it aside or neglecting it altogether? Are you fighting to create your own purpose and plan for your life rather than surrendering to the eternal design of your omniscient heavenly Father? You can be sure that He isn't frustrated or confused by your present situation, nor is He behind schedule.

A TIME FOR

*Reflection*

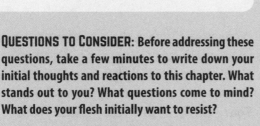

*God never moves without purpose or plan,*
*When trying His servant and molding a man.*
*Oh, rejoice in the Lord! He makes no mistake,*
*He knoweth the end of each path that I take.*
*For when I am tried and purified,*
*I shall come forth as gold.*[19]

**QUESTIONS TO CONSIDER: Before addressing these questions, take a few minutes to write down your initial thoughts and reactions to this chapter. What stands out to you? What questions come to mind? What does your flesh initially want to resist?**

1. How does your perspective change by knowing that God intentionally planted you rather than randomly placing you? What does this teach you about God's thoughts toward you?

2. Where do you seek to plant yourself in life? How does this affect the details of your life, your relationship with God, and how you handle things?

3. Where has God planted you? Are you resisting His placement in any way? Have you ever thought that He made a mistake? If so, when, where, and how?

4. In what areas are you trying to invite God into your plans rather than investing your life in His plan?

5. Do you ever wish you could be in the position of someone else? Why do you wish this?

6. In the garden of your life, have you planted things that God wants uprooted?

7. Consider the fact that God has planted you. What might your life look like if you were to thrive spiritually?

Notes

# THE *Pace* OF THE BLESSED MAN

**PSALM 1:1-3**    *Blessed is the man who walks not in the counsel of the wicked, nor stands in the way of sinners, nor sits in the seat of scoffers; but his delight is in the law of the Lord, and on His law he meditates day and night. He is like a tree planted* **by streams of water** *that yields its fruit in its season, and its leaf does not wither. In all that he does, he prospers.*

**BIG IDEA:**

GOD'S WORD FLOWS AT A CONSISTENT, CONTINUOUS **PACE**, PROVIDING NOURISHMENT RATHER THAN DESTRUCTION— NOTHING LIKE THE RUSHING RIVERS OR THE SQUALID CESSPOOLS OF THE WORLD.

The scene is embedded in my mind.

We were making our way down a remote river to spend time and to teach in a few interior Peruvian villages. The water was unusually high due to recent torrential downfalls. It was hard *not* to be astounded by the fact that some banks of the river had disappeared under the flowing water, while other banks were breaking off from the shore as we motored by them. Many of the remaining trees were precariously clutching the bank with only a few lingering root strands. It almost seemed as though we were characters in a video game as we navigated the river to dodge the floating trees and other jungle debris.

I thought of Psalm 1 and the **pace** of the blessed man. Why pace? *Pace* is "the consistent and continuous speed of a movement" (whether it is someone walking or running, or simply something moving). In the context of our boat trip, the pace of the river was what caused roots to be ripped from the soil and the riverbank to be sucked right into the flowing water.

Originally, I had memorized Psalm 1:3 in the New King James Version, so those were the words that came to mind as I watched the rushing river. *"He shall be like a tree planted by the* **rivers** *of water."* My initial thought was, "Wait. This is *not* a good thing! I'm not sure that I want to be like a tree planted by rivers of water. If God's river is anything like what I'm seeing, uprooting trees and all, how can it possibly be a good thing? How could my life ever survive the pace of God's river?"

But I was missing something.

The word translated in some versions as *river* is translated in others as *stream*. So which one is correct? The Hebrew word is *peleg*. It is translated both as *river* and *stream*, but there is a key to help us understand.

> **The main words used in the**
> **Old Testament Scriptures for *river* are:**
>
> | *ye'or* (an Egyptian word) and *nahar* • used in relation to the Nile, Euphrates, Tigris | *nahal* (not *nahar*) • used for seasonal rivers created during a rainy season |
> |---|---|
>
> **When the Word of God speaks of a normal river,**
> ***peleg* is not the word used.**

But! In Psalm 1:3 we *do* find the word *peleg*.

This word is used only ten times in all of Scripture. Interestingly, it's used almost as often to describe the flow of tears on someone's face or the emotions in someone's heart as it is to describe flowing water. **We might describe it as a babbling brook that has its own source, bubbling up constantly, consistently, gently.** We find it in Isaiah 32:2—*"rivers of water in a dry place."*

In other words, even in an environment where other things are not thriving, this tree is not affected by what's happening upstream. It relies on a source of its own, where the water bubbles up. The pace of this stream, its flow and its speed, are continuous and consistent. This is great news for God's children! God doesn't plant us by rivers that rip us up and dump us into the water when uninvited things happen upstream. Rather, He connects us to a source of nourishment which flows from a much deeper and invisible source that man can't manipulate, that circumstances can't control, and that environment can't eradicate.

> EVEN IN AN ENVIRONMENT WHERE OTHER THINGS ARE NOT THRIVING, THIS TREE IS NOT AFFECTED BY WHAT'S HAPPENING UPSTREAM.

Where are we finding our nourishment? Rather than drawing from the stream of God's Word, are we choosing to walk, stand, and sit by the cesspools of the world? Do we prefer to let the rushing river of the opinions, reviews, and ever-changing news of society carry us along in fret, fear, and unfulfillment? How easily we can become overwhelmed by the pace of this world.

*What pace of life is controlling you?*

• academics?   • expectations?   • careers?
• relationships?   • technology?   • all of the above?

Make a certain grade. Be married by a certain age. Climb the promotion ladder. Save for retirement. From birth to death, this world's pace is relentless—*and increasing.*

But there is a better way.

The blessed man doesn't follow the world's schedule. His success or failure is not defined by the approval or applause of society. He doesn't measure success by the expectations or the pace of the world around him. Rather, he is like a tree planted by constant, consistent, gentle, bubbly streams of water. His steady priority is to respond to God's Word. Daily. Moment by moment.

**THE BLESSED MAN IS LIKE A TREE. HIS STEADY PRIORITY IS TO RESPOND TO GOD'S WORD. DAILY. MOMENT BY MOMENT.**

Naturally, I find it quite easy to look at someone else's life and quickly see (and even suggest) things that need to change. This is not to say that there is never a time to confront another on the dangers of sin in their life. The Word of God clearly teaches us to warn others of God's truth and judgment. But God often convicts me with, *"Seriously? Do I do that to you? If I overwhelmed you with everything in your life that still needs to be conformed to the image of My Son, you would become discouraged. My Word is a lamp to your feet, not a flood-light—enough to show you the next step, not the whole journey. It's a stream intended to give you nourishment and cleansing for today. Just respond today. Then tomorrow allow Me to target what I want to change in you next, one step at a time."*

Our calling is to walk in step with the Word of God. That is His pace. His loving pace.

**SELF-EXAMINATION:** Are you trying to keep pace with the world rather than responding to the pace of the Holy Spirit's conviction in your own life? Are you concentrating on earthly things more than you are listening to conviction concerning eternal things? Are you more concerned with receiving applause from peers than receiving approval from God? God has a pace for you. And as you meditate on His Word day and night, you will be like a tree planted by streams of water. There is no need to feel overwhelmed by life. Just walk in the Spirit. Respond to the pace of the Word, not the pace of the world.

A TIME FOR

*Reflection*

*When we have exhausted our store of endurance,*
*When our strength has failed ere the day is half done,*
*When we reach the end of our hoarded resources,*
*Our Father's full giving is only begun.*
*Fear not that your need shall exceed His provision,*
*Our God ever yearns His resources to share;*
*Lean hard on the arm everlasting, availing;*
*The Father both thee and thy load will upbear.*
*He giveth more grace when the burdens grow greater,*
*He sendeth more strength when the labors increase;*
*To added affliction He addeth His mercy,*
*To multiplied trials, His multiplied peace.*[20]

**QUESTIONS TO CONSIDER:** Before addressing these questions, take a few minutes to write down your initial thoughts and reactions to this chapter. What stands out to you? What questions come to mind? What does your flesh initially want to resist?

1. Where do you feel as though the pace of your life is ripping things apart? What is driving that river?

2. What areas of your life are dictated by the world's expected pace (versus the pace of God's Word)?

3. How would your life change if it were controlled more by the pace of God's Word and less by the pace of your (or someone else's) expectations?

4. Where in life are you trying to catch up to others instead of simply being led by the conviction of the Holy Spirit?

5. The pace of the world can easily affect the mindset of the Church. How has the world's pace infiltrated the Church's view of evangelism, discipleship, money, or even relationships? In what areas are you walking in sync with the expected pace of Christian society rather than in step-by-step obedience to the Lord and His Word?

6. Do you respond to God's Word daily? How might slowing down and being still help to recalibrate you to the pace God has intended for you?

7. It's difficult to walk step by step with the Lord when we are expecting to rush forward by leaps and bounds. Are there areas in your life where you want God to hurry up or to slow down, where you're not at peace with God's pace?

# Notes

_____
_____
_____
_____
_____
_____
_____
_____
_____
_____
_____
_____
_____
_____
_____
_____
_____
_____

# THE *Placement* OF THE BLESSED MAN

**PSALM 1:1-3**    *Blessed is the man who walks not in the counsel of the wicked, nor stands in the way of sinners, nor sits in the seat of scoffers; but his delight is in the law of the Lord, and on His law he meditates day and night. He is **like a tree planted by streams of water** that yields its fruit in its season, and its leaf does not wither. In all that he does, he prospers.*

**BIG IDEA:**

GOD HAS **PLACED** YOU WHERE YOU ARE SO THAT YOU MIGHT GLORIFY HIM IN THAT PRECISE PLACE.

Do you ever feel like your place in God's plan is insignificant? Do you ever see your work as inconsequential? Do you ever consider your life irrelevant? Have you, a close friend, or a loved one gone through some life experience that was filled with intense grief and a pain so deep and real, yet it was unknown to nearly everyone? Know this: God's placement of your life is perfect and purposeful. How might knowing this reality change your life?

In stepping up to get a closer look at this picture of a tree, we saw its powerlessness apart from the outside sources of soil, saturation, and sunlight. We noted the plan in place, recognizing that this tree was planted intentionally, not tossed randomly. We gave some thought to the tree's pace, considering that it was planted by streams of water, not by a powerful river that might sooner or later uproot it. Now we focus our eyes to notice the placement of this tree, the **placement** of the blessed man.

The Scripture says, *"by streams of water."*

This tree is not in Central Park or Stanley Park, nor is it in the yard of the Vatican or Buckingham Palace. This tree is not planted in any place of prominence. Rather, it is a tree planted by streams of water. **The important thing about trees planted by streams of water is not where they aren't planted, but rather where they *are* planted**. Again, this is a picture of a person who meditates on God's Word day and night.

I have a random practice.

When I'm walking by a meadow or a field, or hiking a trail, I like to stop and deviate into the brush. Trekking a little way in, I'll find a random wildflower, lily, or daisy embedded in the grass, and I'll gently pluck it. After admiring its intricacy and its garment of beauty—its patterns, fragrance, and majestic colors—I'll usually choose a few more and take them home to my wife, where we'll put the bouquet into some water to display their beauty until they fade. This might seem a little strange, but I tell you this in order to make an observation and to pose a question.

**My observation is this:** If I hadn't deviated from the path, that flower most likely would have existed and died without ever having one human eye look upon its beauty, smell its fragrance, or appreciate its intricacies. **Thus, my question:** Why does it exist? Oh friend, it exists for the glory of God! Jesus specifically tells us, *"God...clothes the grass of the field"* (Matthew 6:30). A recurring theme in Scripture is that all creation declares the glory of God. And how does this apply to Psalm 1?

How often I have trekked on wilderness trails in magnificent places, like Alaska or New Zealand, passing by thousands of trees planted by streams of water without once stopping to consider their existence. These spectacular trees are rarely noticed individually, but their presence creates an ambience of beauty to be enjoyed by any who venture into their world.

My heart aches, really aches, for my friends who have carried babies only to lose their little ones before any eye ever soaked in the sweetness of their adorable face, any mouth oohed and aahed over their similarities to their parents, or any ear tuned in to their earnest cry to be promptly fed. Yet we must ask, though no one was given the opportunity to see this little flower face-to-face, was the life of this little one any less valuable? Not in the least. She or he was created for the glory of God, and, in God's sovereignty and mercy, He chose to give that little one a very brief time inside their mother's womb.

Maybe the place in which you have been planted and called to be faithful feels much like a concealed womb. Perhaps you feel like a random flower in a forgotten field or a tree planted by a stream of water. Perhaps the prayer closet is your primary place of residence.

**IS THERE ANY HIGHER CALLING THAN THAT OF CAMPING OUT IN THE PRESENCE OF GOD?**

But is there any higher calling than that of camping out in the presence of God? Is your isolated place in the service of the elderly or in the care of the young? Maybe you've remained at the bedside of a loved one for a very long time, watching years—your years—go by as you care daily for them. If so, don't forget the words of Jesus in Matthew 10:42, *"And whoever gives one of these little ones even a cup of cold water because he is a disciple, truly, I say to you, he will by no means lose his reward."* **Do not focus on the tree-gazers, but on the tree's Gardener.** He has you where He wants you—in His law and enjoying His love.

**SELF-EXAMINATION:** You may feel unseen by most, unimportant to the masses, and unappreciated by society, but my friend, remember this: It isn't where you're not placed that matters. What matters is Who put you where you are. Are you discontent with your current placement? Are you wasting time wishing to be elsewhere rather than worshiping the One who placed you exactly where He wants you? If God has placed you at home caring for children, don't stoop to becoming CEO of a company. If God has directed you to take the gospel to Wall Street, don't be envious of the one He has sent to plant churches in a foreign land.

A TIME FOR

*Reflection*

*Does the place you're called to labor*
*Seem so small and little known?*
*It is great if God is in it, and He'll not forget His own.*
*When the conflict here is ended,*
*And our race on earth is run,*
*He will say, if we are faithful,*
*'Welcome home, My child—well done!'*
*Little is much when God is in it.*
*Labor not for wealth or fame.*
*There's a crown and you can win it,*
*If you go in Jesus' Name.*[21]

**QUESTIONS TO CONSIDER: Before addressing these questions, take a few minutes to write down your initial thoughts and reactions to this chapter. What stands out to you? What questions come to mind? What does your flesh initially want to resist?**

1. Where has God planted you (not necessarily geographically, but among lives, in situations, etc.)?

2. What placement of a life (your own life, or perhaps someone else's) by God might you tend to view as *insignificant? Inconsequential?* Why might you see these things the way you do?

3. What event or placement of your life, unseen by others, might God have intentionally entrusted to you for your growth? Take a few minutes to journal the significance of His placement of this particular circumstance in your life.

4. Is there a place of your planting that you question or are currently discontented with?

5. What situations have you experienced where the purpose for the pain wasn't (and maybe still isn't) clear? How can you glorify God in the unknown?

6. In what areas of your life are you focused on tree-gazers rather than on the tree's Gardener? Explain.

7. Describe a time in your life when you experienced the reality of *Little Is Much When God Is in It,* a time when the smallest act or detail led to something far greater.

Notes

# THE *Progression* OF THE BLESSED MAN

**PSALM 1:1-3** *Blessed is the man who walks not in the counsel of the wicked, nor stands in the way of sinners, nor sits in the seat of scoffers; but his delight is in the law of the Lord, and on His law he meditates day and night. He is **like a tree planted by streams of water** that yields its fruit in its season, and its leaf does not wither. In all that he does, he prospers.*

**BIG IDEA:**

MATURITY IS A STEP-BY-STEP **PROGRESSION**. THE ONE WHO MEDITATES DAY AND NIGHT WILL PRODUCE WHOLESOME FRUIT IN DUE TIME.

When diving into Scripture, we see examples of prophets like Abraham, who was called *"a friend of God"* (James 2:23); David, whom God labeled *"a man after My heart"* (Acts 13:22); and Moses, whom *"the Lord knew face to face"* (Deuteronomy 34:10). After reading of these individuals, we can easily feel disillusioned by where we find ourselves in our own spiritual journey. We might wonder why we aren't further along in spiritual maturity or perceived usefulness. Take heart, my friend. This journey doesn't begin with maturity in our walk; it begins with meditation in His Word. But when we choose to respond to God's Word in obedience, spiritual maturity will be the result.

Take a closer look at the blessed man's *progression.*

In looking at our own lives, we commonly believe that if we can get to a certain point in our faith, *then* God will use us. This is a lie of the enemy aimed at keeping us from obeying *today*. Obedience to the Lord and usefulness in His work aren't put on hold until *tomorrow*. There is a progression in our walk with Christ, and each step that we take is to be a decisive step in response to His Word—today.

In Psalm 1:3, we are told that the blessed man *"is like a tree planted by streams of water."* Notice where the tree begins, its starting point. Planted. It is a planted tree. It is not a mature tree, not a massive tree, not even a fruitful tree. If you plant a sapling, you don't expect it to grow fruit for you that year. It is not in the fruit-bearing stage, nor will it be very soon. There is a progression in the life-cycle of a tree, and we see that progression as we walk through verse three.

**YOU RECOGNIZE THAT GROWTH TAKES TIME. SO TOO WE MUST RECOGNIZE THAT THE LORD HAS A PLANNED PROGRESSION FOR EACH STAGE OF OUR LIVES.**

You don't likely look at a seed or a sapling and say, "Wow, that's an unsuccessful venture." You recognize that growth takes time. So too we must recognize that the Lord has a planned progression for each stage of our lives. Yet how natural it is for us to try to judge our own effectiveness rather than to simply respond in obedience. The one who meditates day and night is planted by the stream. That meditation doesn't bring immediate maturity, but it does lead to healthy growth. Keep in mind, we all desire that the line-graph of our lives would reveal a steady, positive rise of continual growth, but even trees do not always show such a pattern. There may be days and seasons where growth is exponential, but the reality of our lives will more than likely be a jagged line of progression.

When I was a boy, I was sad nearly every time my height was measured, not because I was short for my age, but because I was the shortest among my siblings, being the youngest of three by a couple of years. It didn't matter to me at the time that I was taller than they had been at that stage of life. Instead, I was traumatized that I never seemed to catch up. I was evaluating growth based on comparison. Not a good idea. (As a side note, today I'm half a foot taller than my siblings.) Measuring an oak tree against a moringa tree is not a fair comparison. They have different structures, patterns, purposes, and fruit. So it is with those who walk with the Lord.

The type of tree in Psalm 1 is not specified. All we need to know is that it was intended to produce the fruit the Divine Gardener had in mind. That is why He planted it.

Still, there is *another* exciting spiritual truth in the planting of this tree.

The Hebrew word translated as *planted* is *shathal*. This word specifically denotes a *transplanting* of a tree. This is a fabulous realization. We have not only been planted, but we have been transplanted. To transplant means that something has been "moved or transferred from one place or situation to another." For us as believers, it indicates that we were previously growing elsewhere, but God has moved us to a new place of growth.

> **WE HAVE NOT ONLY BEEN *PLANTED*, BUT WE HAVE BEEN *TRANSPLANTED*. FOR US AS BELIEVERS, IT INDICATES THAT WE WERE PREVIOUSLY GROWING ELSEWHERE, BUT GOD HAS MOVED US TO A NEW PLACE OF GROWTH.**

Consider Colossians 1:13 where we are told that God has *"delivered us from the domain of darkness and transferred* [transplanted] *us to the kingdom of His beloved Son."* We are not merely planted; we are transplanted. As we saw last time, our progression begins with our placement by the Master Gardener. Then there is a progression from being planted to being productive. Christ-likeness isn't a quick, overnight process. It is, and will continue to be, a constant progression and continual pursuit until we are at last in His presence in complete perfection. John reminds his disciples, *"We know that when He appears we shall be like Him, because we shall see Him as He is. And everyone who thus hopes in Him purifies himself as He is pure"* (1 John 3:2-3).

Don't be discouraged with where you are, but be diligent to respond daily to His law, His Word, and to His heart. Let's not settle into complacency or be satisfied with mediocrity, but may we neither become disheartened when our rate of growth fails to meet our expectations. Remember, the only seed that sprang up *quickly* in Jesus' parable of the sower and the soils (Matthew 13, Mark 4, Luke 8) was the seed which fell on rocky soil. What happened to it? It was quickly scorched and died. Quick growth isn't necessarily healthy growth.

**LET'S NOT SETTLE INTO COMPLACENCY. BUT MAY WE NEITHER BECOME DISHEARTENED WHEN OUR RATE OF GROWTH FAILS TO MEET OUR EXPECTATIONS.**

**SELF-EXAMINATION:** Are you discouraged with where you find yourself in your walk with Christ? Are you discouraged with the placement, pace, or progression of your own life? Allow me to ask you: With whom are you comparing yourself? What step of obedience would Christ have you take today toward knowing Him more intimately? Is there any step of obedience to God which you are delaying to take because you don't deem yourself worthy or qualified? Remember, He is at work and will finish what He has started in you.

A TIME FOR

*Reflection*

> *Little by little, every day,*
> *Little by little in every way,*
> *My Jesus is changing me.*
> *Since I made that turnabout face,*
> *I've been growing in His grace,*
> *My Jesus is changing me.*
> *I'm not the same person that I used to be.*
> *Sometimes it's slow going, but there's a knowing*
> *That, someday, perfect I will be.*[22]

**QUESTIONS TO CONSIDER:** Before addressing these questions, take a few minutes to write down your initial thoughts and reactions to this chapter. What stands out to you? What questions come to mind? What does your flesh initially want to resist?

1. In what areas of your spiritual life are you discouraged by your lack of growth?

2. It can be good to take note of other examples, but are you comparing yourself with anyone else? Who are you comparing yourself with? Why? How might this be detrimental to your spiritual growth?

3. Why might it be significant that the type of tree is not mentioned in Psalm 1?

4. Take some time to meditate on God's Word. What might be the next step of obedience for you to take today? Remember, obedience should *not* be based on your perception of which command is of greatest importance. To give thanks in everything is as much a command of Scripture as is the command to go into all the world and make disciples.

5. When you consider progression in your life, is Christlikeness your aim? Or busyness for Christ? Give examples.

6. Have you grown complacent in your walk with Christ? The blessed man is on a journey of progression; he is not sitting in stagnation. Where are you prematurely content in your relationship with Christ (where Christ would have you to enter into deeper intimacy with Him)?

7. What does spiritual growth look like to you? Is your view of spiritual growth biblical? Are you concerned about how other people view your spiritual growth, or are you concerned with growing in your relationship with Christ and in aiming to please Him?

# Notes

## THE *Privacy* OF THE BLESSED MAN

**PSALM 1:1-3**   *Blessed is the man who walks not in the counsel of the wicked, nor stands in the way of sinners, nor sits in the seat of scoffers; but his delight is in the law of the Lord, and on His law he meditates day and night. He is **like a tree planted** by streams of water that yields its fruit in its season, and its leaf does not wither. In all that he does, he prospers.*

**BIG IDEA:**

INTIMACY WITH GOD IS A RESULT OF THE **PRIVACY** OF THE SECRET PLACE, NOT OF OUR PERFORMANCE ON THE SOCIAL PLATFORM.

hat if everything in my walk with God were taken away except the parts that no one else can see? If all the external practices of my faith were removed, *what would be left?* Gone are the public church services. Gone are the prayers made before others. Gone are the social media posts. Gone are the times when I've talked about God when I was with Christian friends.

Not that any of these are negative things, but play the game—*and just imagine.* What if all that was left in your relationship with God were the times you sought Him in secret?

Give it some serious thought.

Now consider the **privacy** of the blessed man. The text reminds us that this man *"is like a tree planted by streams of water."* So we ask, "Where is the strength of a tree found?" Think this through. No matter how beautiful a tree may be, its strength

**WHAT IF ALL THAT WAS LEFT IN YOUR RELATIONSHIP WITH GOD WERE THE TIMES YOU SOUGHT HIM IN SECRET?**

will not be found in the color of its leaves, the size of its fruit, or the fullness of its branches. A tree's strength is hidden away in a part which no one sees. The strength of a tree is determined by the depth, breadth, and health of its root system.

Consider this thoughtfully. The strength of a tree lies in the part that no one sees. **Privacy**.

**CONSIDER THIS THOUGHTFULLY. THE STRENGTH OF A TREE LIES IN THE PART THAT NO ONE SEES. PRIVACY.**

This is a powerful spiritual picture. In Jeremiah 17:7-8, we are told, *"Blessed is the man who trusts in the Lord, whose trust is the Lord. He is like a tree planted by water, that sends out its roots by the stream, and does not fear when heat comes, for its leaves remain green, and is not anxious in the year of drought, for it does not cease to bear fruit."* In Ephesians 3:17, Paul prays that Christians would be *"rooted and grounded in love."* Again, in Colossians 2:6-7, *"Therefore, as you received Christ Jesus the Lord, so walk in Him, rooted and built up in Him and established in the faith, just as you were taught, abounding in thanksgiving."*

Go back in your minds to the parable of the soils. Earlier in our journey, we referred to the second soil, the rocky ground. In Matthew 13:6, Jesus warned, *"But when the sun rose they were scorched. And since they had no root, they withered away."* Then in Matthew 13:21, *"Yet he has no root in himself, but endures for a while, and when tribulation or persecution arises on account of the word, immediately he falls away."* The issue was not the heat of the sun which is, of course, essential to growth. The *root* of the problem was a *root* problem!

**THE ROOT OF THE PROBLEM WAS A ROOT PROBLEM! THE CRISIS [COMES] FROM GROWTH WITHOUT DEPTH.**

The crisis came from growth without depth. But if shallowness has been your experience, take heart. God invites you now to plunge your roots deep into the fertile soil of His Word.

When we are rooted in the eternal, we will not be threatened when tribulation or persecution comes. And, just as the sun in the parable seemed to be a threat but was actually necessary for growth, tribulation or persecution will in our case prove to be a conduit of greater blessing and reward. Check out Matthew 5:10-12. **Tribulation is only a threat when we see our earthly life as the prize.**

Are we rooted in the eternal Word of God or in the temporary, turbulent world of trends? How often our Savior sought solitude and silence by camping out in the presence of His Father. Our relationship with God is not strengthened by our eloquence of speech, by the clothes we wear to public gatherings, or by the quality of our music during times of worship. Our success is not measured by our church attendance record, by the approval or affirmation of others, or by how well we know how to act as a Christian. Rather, our true strength lies in a place that no other human can see.

**HOW OFTEN OUR SAVIOR SOUGHT SOLITUDE AND SILENCE BY CAMPING OUT IN THE PRESENCE OF HIS FATHER.**

This is important.

In most cases, the exposure of a tree's roots is a negative thing and could indicate some form of erosion. That erosion is a good illustration of the danger of spiritual pride. When we seek to reveal our roots, we do not prove our strength but, rather, expose our weakness. In contrast, the blessed man, the one whose roots are deeply grounded in God's Word, feels no need to show his roots. His life will inevitably reveal the reality of his day and night meditation on the Word of God. As Jesus noted in Matthew 5:16, *"In the same way, let your light shine before others, so that they may see your good works and give glory to your Father who is in heaven."* This is the rooted life where *fruit* is evident to all since the *roots* run deep in God's Word.

**THE BLESSED MAN FEELS NO NEED TO SHOW HIS ROOTS. HIS LIFE WILL INEVITABLY REVEAL THE REALITY OF HIS DAY AND NIGHT MEDITATION ON THE WORD OF GOD.**

**Intimacy with God is a result of the secret place, not of our performance on the social platform.** It has *no* dependence on pride, preferences, prestige, pedestals, and preeminence of personal position. It is found, rather, in surrender, submission, and solitude with and service to the Savior.

Keep Christ's exhortations of Matthew 6 close in your thoughts. On giving, Jesus taught, *"But when you give to the needy, do not let your left hand know what your right hand is doing, so that your giving may be in secret. And your Father who sees in secret will reward you"* (Matthew 6:3-4). Here we see the privacy of the blessed man.

**WHEN JESUS TAUGHT ON GIVING, PRAYER, AND FASTING, HE SAID: "DO IT IN SECRET." AND HE SAID, "YOUR FATHER WHO SEES IN SECRET WILL REWARD YOU."**

When Jesus taught on prayer, what did He say? *"But when you pray, go into your room and shut the door and pray to your Father who is in secret. And your Father who sees in secret will reward you"* (Matthew 6:6). Again, we see the privacy of the blessed man.

When Jesus taught on fasting, He made this same point a third time: *"But when you fast, anoint your head and wash your face, that your fasting may not be seen by others but by your Father who is in secret. And your Father who sees in secret will reward you"* (Matthew 6:17-18). Once again, we see the privacy of the blessed man.

> **Roots might not be visible,
> but the results of a rooted believer
> cannot be hidden.**

TURN THE PAGE
FOR A TIME OF
*Reflection*

**SELF-EXAMINATION:** Does the fruit of your life glorify your Savior or yourself? Do people leave conversations with you impressed with you or impressed with your God? What would be left in your relationship with God should every publicly shared part of your faith-life be gone today? God shares His glory with no one. When you get the glory, He doesn't (see Isaiah 42:8). Are you a thief of God's glory? Am I? May our light so shine before people that they leave our presence having tasted of God's goodness and glory.

A TIME FOR

*Reflection*

> Just a channel full of blessing,
> To the thirsty hearts around,
> To tell out Thy full salvation,
> All Thy loving message sound.
>
> Channels only, blessed Master,
> But with all Thy loving power,
> Flowing through us,
> Thou canst use us,
> Every day and every hour.[23]

**QUESTIONS TO CONSIDER: Before addressing these questions, take a few minutes to write down your initial thoughts and reactions to this chapter. What stands out to you? What questions come to mind? What does your flesh initially want to resist?**

1. If all your "public" Christian life were stripped away, what would your walk with God look like?

2. From what source, other than the Word of God, are the roots of your life drawing strength?

3. Are you more concerned with what others think of you than you are with the pursuit of God's work in you?

4. Do you treat the Word differently in public than you do in private? How does your private prayer life differ from your public prayers?

5. Journal these answers privately: Are you actively seeking the secret place in His presence? Do you spend time with the Lord when no one else can see? Do you feel totally satisfied that the Lord knows your situation even when you can't share it publicly?

6. What is your motivation behind the public statements that you make? Is it to impress others or to magnify God? Is it an outpouring of what God is teaching you in the secret place?

7. What are some practical ways to test your motivation before you speak or act publicly?

## Notes

# THE *Pattern* OF THE BLESSED MAN

> **PSALM 1:1-3**  *Blessed is the man who walks not in the counsel of the wicked, nor stands in the way of sinners, nor sits in the seat of scoffers; but his delight is in the law of the Lord, and on His law he meditates day and night. He is **like a tree planted** by streams of water that yields its fruit in its season, and its leaf does not wither. In all that he does, he prospers.*

**BIG IDEA:**

THE IDEAL TIME TO DEVELOP A **PATTERN** FOR HEALTHY ABSORPTION AND GROWTH IS WHILE YOUR ROOTS ARE YOUNG AND TENDER.

atterns.

A pattern is a model or a design used as a guide. Who uses them? All kinds of people, from software engineers to quilters. I distinctly remember an activity from my childhood in which we would make plastic canvas yarn pictures by sewing directly onto a pattern. Following the pattern produced the picture shown on the box. When God's Spirit directed and inspired the psalmist to pen this first psalm, He chose the picture of a tree as a simile for the blessed man. And so this tree is the *pattern* that God would have us consider, learn from, and follow.

Our pattern, or guide, is that of a *healthy tree*. If we choose to follow God's pattern, the blessed life will be the result. Let's focus on the roots of the tree and look at three aspects of God's pattern for roots. Since I'm no arborist, I consulted outside sources to understand healthy root patterns.[24]

**OUR PATTERN, OR GUIDE, IS THAT OF A *HEALTHY TREE*.**

I learned that roots have two main purposes: (1) to absorb nutrients for the tree, and (2) to anchor the tree.

**Absorb, then anchor. Absorb, then anchor.** If these two things take place as intended, a third element will also materialize: (3) to affect. When we absorb as we ought, we will be anchored as we require, and we will affect others as we might. So we ask: What are we absorbing? Where are we anchored? How are we affecting others?

**WHEN WE ABSORB AS WE OUGHT, WE WILL BE ANCHORED AS WE REQUIRE, AND WE WILL AFFECT OTHERS AS WE MIGHT.**

A tree's roots absorb water and nutrients. About this, the National Arboretum states, *"Most of the nutrients taken into the tree are absorbed by young roots. Old roots are tough and woody, anchoring the tree."* Did you allow that to soak into your mind? Read it again. Young roots will absorb most of the nutrients a tree will receive. How vital are those early decisions of life! The choices we make in our youth, or in the youth of our faith, establish patterns that tend to be fixed for life. In the words of Solomon, *"Remember also your Creator in the days of your youth, before the evil days come and the years draw near of which you will say, 'I have no pleasure in them'"* (Ecclesiastes 12:1).

### Take this warning to heart...

Perhaps you are absorbing content unbeknown to any other human being—only you and God are aware of it. You're caught in an addiction of absorption that is anchoring you to the worthless elements of the world. I'm not just referring to pornography, prescription drugs, illegal activities, or some other form of sinful perversion. I am suggesting that any subtle lure of this world is a potential source of absorption which may lead to spiritual decay.

**ANY SUBTLE LURE OF THIS WORLD IS A POTENTIAL SOURCE OF ABSORPTION WHICH MAY LEAD TO SPIRITUAL DECAY.**

Perhaps you are more absorbed with your body and physical health than you are with your soul and spiritual health. Perhaps you are obsessed with promoting a new diet or supplement as if it were gospel news. Or perhaps you are a shopaholic, perusing review after review late into the night as you ponder your next purchase. Maybe you're using your precious God-given time and abilities to master a new video game, to meditate on Pinterest more than on God's promises, or to thoughtlessly binge-watch a new season of your favorite distraction, thereby displacing a right preoccupation with eternal things. Or perhaps you're anchoring yourself to academic pursuits at the price of ignoring eternal endeavors that you know God has called you to invest in.

No, I am not saying that *all* these things are bad, but we dare not anchor ourselves to them. Our anchor will be fixed in the same place from which we derive our source of nourishment, whether healthful or harmful. The psalm makes it clear that the blessed man is absorbing God's Word:

**OUR ANCHOR WILL BE FIXED IN THE SAME PLACE FROM WHICH WE DERIVE OUR SOURCE OF NOURISHMENT.**

*"His delight is in the law of the Lord, and on His law He meditates day and night"* (Psalm 1:2). I say this drenched in love: If any of the previous statements offended you, perhaps they were meant for you. Ask yourself, "What is my pattern?"

The blessed man absorbs, absorbs, absorbs. His anchor and its placement are clearly articulated by the writer of Hebrews: *"We have this* [firm hope of God's promises] *as a sure and steadfast anchor of the soul, a hope that enters into the inner place behind the curtain"* (Hebrews 6:19). Going back, did you notice what the arboretum said about absorption versus anchoring? Most absorption takes place early on in a tree's life because, the older the tree, the rougher and tougher the roots. This does *not* negate the marvelous grace of Jesus Christ that softens hard, calloused hearts, but, to those who ignore the warning, beware!

How vital it is to decide *now* to root your life deeply in the Word of God, lest your heart be deceived by the passing pleasures of sin and the compromising nature of culture and complacency.

**HOW VITAL IT IS TO DECIDE NOW TO ROOT YOUR LIFE DEEPLY IN THE WORD OF GOD.**

But what about the third component? We have seen that roots have two main purposes: (1) to **absorb** nutrients for the tree, and (2) to **anchor** the tree. But we also need to understand that (3) the roots of a tree **affect** their environment, whether for benefit or for harm. If a disease infects a tree's root system, that disease can infiltrate the soil and bring death to other trees nearby. Conversely, healthy trees will nourish the surrounding soil with beneficial nutrients, will prevent soil erosion by their extensive roots, will act as wind-breakers, and will play a significant role in the water cycle. Just think, all these far-reaching effects from a single tree.

So, the health of a tree's root system clearly affects its environment, either positively *or negatively*. The effects of a single tree's roots are not limited to that single tree. What a lesson to take to heart!

**SELF-EXAMINATION:** We have a pattern to follow. What we absorb reveals where our anchor is fixed. Where we are anchored will affect those around us. Today, what are you absorbing? Each and every day that we fail to absorb the nutrients that profit the soul results in a weakening of the health of our root system.

A TIME FOR

*Reflection*

How are you affecting lives around you? When you leave your office, your home, an appointment, or a conversation, what fills the thoughts of those you were just with? In what direction did your influence steer them? Did it nudge them toward things of eternal value or toward matters that are ultimately inconsequential? Are there some roots that need to be cut right out of your life? The Word of God tells us to let the mind of Christ be our mind (See Philippians 2:5). This means that we are to think as Jesus thinks. May we absorb His Word and be firmly anchored in who He is and what He has done so that all those around us might be affected, for time and for eternity, by the hidden *healthy* roots of our life.

> O Lord, I'm just a tree in You / Rooted and being built in You,
> Absorbing all You are to me / What a place to be! [25]

**QUESTIONS TO CONSIDER:** Before addressing these questions, take a few minutes to write down your initial thoughts and reactions to this chapter. What stands out to you? What questions come to mind? What does your flesh initially want to resist?

1. What have you absorbed in the past twenty-four hours?

2. What do you absorb on a day-to-day basis that contradicts the Word of God? (This is not an indictment of sin but a call to take inventory.)

3. We are anchored to what we regularly absorb. To what ideas, fads, obsessions, or doctrines are we presently anchored?

4. To what and to whom we are anchored will affect those around us. How are our absorption tendencies affecting the lives of others?

5. How are the absorption tendencies of those around you affecting your life? Give an example, but recognize that this is not an excuse for you to imitate any patterns of ungodliness.

6. Make a list of the people whose influence (positive or negative) you are choosing to absorb (artists, celebrities, bloggers, vloggers, theologians, friends, family, etc.). Be specific. How might some of their ideas be harmfully infecting your roots? Do these influences cause you to treasure Jesus Christ more?

7. What is the difference in your attitude on days when you primarily absorb what the world is saying versus the days when you filter everything through the law of the Lord? Describe the difference that choice makes in your mindset, your priorities, and your actions.

Notes

# THE *Pain* OF THE BLESSED MAN

**PSALM 1:1-3**   *Blessed is the man who walks not in the counsel of the wicked, nor stands in the way of sinners, nor sits in the seat of scoffers; but his delight is in the law of the Lord, and on His law he meditates day and night. He is **like a tree planted** by streams of water that yields its fruit in its season, and its leaf does not wither. In all that he does, he prospers.*

**BIG IDEA:**

ADVERSITY STRENGTHENS US AS THE **PAIN** THAT WE EXPERIENCE IN HARD TIMES CAUSES US TO PUSH OUR ROOTS DEEPER INTO THE LORD.

This discussion is often avoided in the church, but, until it's embraced, I believe we will miss out on the intimacy God offers us. Let's look again at the roots of this tree as we investigate the **pain** of the blessed life. While we all encounter pain, perhaps we have not all learned to accept it as an opportunity from God. Do we frequently see pain as a problem we need to avoid or be rid of rather than a precious proffer by God to welcome His work in us?

Think about this. Roots.

We saw the privacy of roots, as well as their pattern, but how do roots grow strong? Some trees have root systems of great breadth, like the redwoods in California. These trees can reach a height of over 350 feet, and, though their root system may run only six feet deep, it can extend to 100 feet wide, often intertwining itself with the roots of other Redwoods.[26] In contrast, there's a wild fig tree in South Africa whose roots measure more than 400 feet deep.[27]

But *how* do roots grow strong, deep, or wide? In the late 1980s, a study was carried out which involved the creation of a biosphere, named *Biosphere 2*, the presumed ideal setting for plant life and human existence. And, you know, it really did seem perfect. When the experiment began, things grew wonderfully in the biosphere. However, over time, a problem surfaced. Some trees would grow to a certain height and then simply topple over. What did scientists discover to be the cause? A lack of adversity! To grow strong, full roots, trees need adversity. They need wind and storms. Sure, the trees looked beautiful and healthy, but their roots had no true strength because they had been deprived of adverse conditions.[28] This is a foundational truth: A tree planted by streams of water may have ideal conditions of soil, saturation, and sunlight—but it also needs **strain**.

**WHAT DID SCIENTISTS DISCOVER TO BE THE CAUSE [OF POOR PLANT GROWTH]? A LACK OF ADVERSITY!**

As we meditate on the law of the Lord day and night, we increase in the knowledge of Him, and our roots broaden. But it is only as we experience the Lord in hard times that our roots push deeper into Him. It only makes sense. If you want to know God as your Comforter, would you expect Him to infuse you with mere knowledge, or would you expect Him to provide you with experiences in which you get to taste His comfort? To truly know Him as your Comforter requires that He allows you to experience grief or distress. Similarly, to know Him as your Healer requires disease and pain. To know Him as your Strength requires that you feel your own weakness (so that you

**IT IS ONLY AS WE EXPERIENCE THE LORD IN HARD TIMES THAT OUR ROOTS PUSH DEEPER INTO HIM. IT ONLY MAKES SENSE.**

might experience His strength made perfect in your weakness). Do you want to know God as your Provider? Expect to find yourself in need and desperation. Do you want to know Him as your Peace? Count on conditions of turmoil and unrest. If you want to know God as your Sustainer, get ready for a phase of prolonged testing. Your Defender and Advocate? Expect false accusations and times of misunderstanding. Finally, if you're ever going to know God as your resurrection, well... prepare to die.

**IF YOU'RE EVER GOING TO KNOW GOD AS YOUR RESURRECTION, WELL... PREPARE TO DIE.**

The important question is this: Do you just want to know a lot *about* God, or do you want to truly know and experience *Him*?

In the Bible, multiple Greek words are translated as *know*. But one word is commonly used for knowing God. It's *ginosko*, which can be defined as *experiential* knowledge. Jesus teaches us in John 14:21 that He manifests, or shows Himself, to those who keep His Word.

My friends, abiding in the Word, and the journey it entails, promises persecution, rejection, and adversity—just the strain we need so that we might develop strong, deep roots. Jesus reminded His disciples, *"If the world hates you, know that it has hated Me before it hated you. If you were of the world, the world would love you as its own; but because you are not of the world, but I chose you out of the world, therefore the world hates you. Remember the word that I said to you, 'A servant is not greater than his master.' If they persecuted Me, they will also persecute you. If they kept My word,*

**ABIDING IN THE WORD PROMISES JUST THE STRAIN WE NEED SO THAT WE MIGHT DEVELOP STRONG, DEEP ROOTS.**

*they will also keep yours"* (John 15:18-20). A little later on, the apostle Paul shared with Timothy, his son in the faith, *"All who desire to live a godly life in Christ Jesus will be persecuted"* (2 Timothy 3:12). No exceptions.

Let me state it in this fashion:

If you want strong roots, if you want the blessed life, adversity is not only the norm—*it is a necessity*. This doesn't mean we look for winds of adversity; *they* will find *us*. Nor does this mean you'll be burned at the stake for Christ. But it does mean that you will suffer. Whether by being misunderstood for Christ's sake, or by resisting temptation and the pull of the world, or by physical torment—the rejection is real. But, through suffering and testing, your roots will develop and grow strong.

**SELF-EXAMINATION:** Do you seek to avoid the storm rather than draw near to the Savior? Are there present situations in your life which you label as obstacles by which God might actually be offering you opportunities for growth in godliness (and deep roots)? **Could it be that God wants to increase your courage rather than change your circumstances?** When you respond positively to the Word, the wind of this world will beat against you. But be encouraged: Those who belong to the Lord will not *only* stand but will also become trees that are sturdy, strong, steady, and satisfying (to others). We need wind, we need adversity, and we need pain. The storms won't last forever, but the blessings reaped from them will. **Remember, the obstacles of this life are eternally valuable opportunities to know Him more and to sink those roots deep into the foundation that never moves** (Hebrews 12:28).

A TIME FOR

*Reflection*

> Sometimes the day seems long, our trials hard to bear;
> We're tempted to complain, to murmur and despair.
> But Christ will soon appear to catch his bride away,
> All tears forever over in God's eternal day!
> It will be worth it all when we see Jesus!
> Life's trials will seem so small when we see Christ.
> One glimpse of His dear face, all sorrow will erase,
> So bravely run the race till we see Christ.[29]

**QUESTIONS TO CONSIDER:** Before addressing these questions, take a few minutes to write down your initial thoughts and reactions to this chapter. What stands out to you? What questions come to mind? What does your flesh initially want to resist?

1. What pain do you currently have in your life? Do you see this as an opportunity or an obstacle? Explain.

2. In what things are you praying that God will change your circumstances rather than praying that He will increase your courage? Not that the former is wrong, but how might God want to change the way you pray?

3. How might God be presently strengthening your roots for future adversity and opportunity?

4. Are there obstacles or "winds" in your life that you see as a hindrance rather than a help for knowing God more deeply?

5. What are some past "pains" where you can now see how God was working in you through it all?

6. In what areas of your life are you valuing knowledge of (or about) God over knowing and experiencing God Himself?

7. We saw how God reveals Himself as our Comforter, Healer, Sustainer, Defender, Provider, and more. Give a few examples of ways in which God has revealed Himself to you in hard times. Are you giving God praise, glory, and thanks for your current situation? What does that look like?

Notes

# THE *Provision* OF THE BLESSED MAN

**PSALM 1:1-3** *Blessed is the man who walks not in the counsel of the wicked, nor stands in the way of sinners, nor sits in the seat of scoffers; but his delight is in the law of the Lord, and on His law he meditates day and night. He is **like a tree planted** by streams of water **that yields its fruit in its season**, and its leaf does not wither. In all that he does, he prospers.*

**BIG IDEA:**

THE SPIRITUAL FRUIT THAT WE BEAR IS A **PROVISION** FOR THOSE AROUND US WHO SO DESPERATELY NEED TO TASTE OF CHRIST.

*I* still remember the conversation. A mentor and I were sitting at a small Chinese restaurant in Niamey, the capital city of Niger, Africa, when he began talking about fruit. He wasn't speaking of pomegranates, oranges, or mangoes, but of things like love, joy, and peace. He then shared a revolutionary thought with me. Perhaps you'll find it simple, but for me it was life-changing.

He said, "I prayed so often for my life to bear fruit, but I figured that meant people getting saved and being transformed around

**THE FRUIT I'M SUPPOSED TO BEAR ISN'T IN *OTHERS*, BUT IN *ME*.**

me. But then I looked at Galatians and noticed that the fruit I'm supposed to bear isn't in others, but in me. And it looked a whole lot like *'love, joy, peace, patience, kindness, goodness, faithfulness, gentleness, and self-control.'*"

It's time for us to consider the **provision** of the blessed man.

In Psalm 1:3 we are told, *"He is like a tree planted by streams of water that yields its fruit in its season."* A tree which *"yields its fruit."* In

**IS A TREE'S FRUIT INTENDED TO BENEFIT THE TREE OR OTHERS?**

order to turn your mind toward the direction we are heading, think through this question: Is a tree's fruit intended to benefit the tree or others? Quite obviously, fruit does not grow for the good of the tree. It's there for others to enjoy. Similarly, the blessed man is a source of provision for others. But let's go further.

This next aspect amazed me as I spent time contemplating it.

A healthy tree bears fruit, but that fruit must be thinned. Thinning is a common process with fruit such as apples or nectarines. It involves removing excess fruit so that the fruit which remains might grow in both size and quality. When a tree's fruit isn't thinned, or when its fruit isn't picked, it not only begins to bear smaller fruit which is neither very useful nor sweet, but worse, the fruit rots, attracting insects and bugs, and potentially causing infection and other problems.

**THINNING INVOLVES REMOVING EXCESS FRUIT SO THAT THE FRUIT WHICH REMAINS MIGHT GROW IN BOTH *SIZE* AND *QUALITY*.**

Are you picturing this?

**Fruit isn't for the tree; it's for others.** And fruit needs to be picked. It needs to be consumed. It needs to be savored and enjoyed. Our bearing of spiritual fruit is meant to be of benefit to the world around us that so desperately needs to taste of Christ. Jesus said to His disciples in John 15:8, *"By this My Father*

*is glorified, that you bear much fruit and so prove to be My disciples."*
The proof is in the tasting.

What is the fruit that we are to bear?

- **Fruit of the Spirit of God.**
- **Fruit that reveals Jesus Christ to the world.**
- **Fruit that glorifies the Father.**

This objective will be life-changing when we willingly absorb
its truth. We normally want to avoid conflict, adversity, and
rejection, but it is *in those very circumstances* that fruit such as
love and patience and self-control become most evident. It is
in those moments that the world will see and taste our fruit and
will be led to exclaim, "Amazing! How can anyone respond in
such a manner?" It whets their appetite for our Savior.

Perhaps you are going through a battle with cancer, but what a
fabulous opportunity to bear fruit. Hope shines brightly when
you rise up in faith instead of sinking in
despair, when the world says, "You have
every reason to be discouraged, down-
trodden, and disillusioned," but you
surprise them instead with the fruit of
the Spirit. The watching world will
benefit from the hope growing on your
branches. We don't produce fruit. We
can't produce it. A tree only *bears* fruit.
As its roots reach deep into the soil by
the stream, fruit can't help but grow. Fruit is the natural yield
of a healthy tree planted by streams of water. So it is for the person of God who has their roots in His Word.

> HOPE SHINES
> BRIGHTLY WHEN YOU
> RISE UP IN FAITH
> INSTEAD OF SINKING
> IN DESPAIR. THE
> WATCHING WORLD
> WILL BENEFIT FROM
> THE HOPE GROWING
> ON YOUR BRANCHES.

It's easy to think of times of abundance and ease in your life as your "seasons of fruit." Sometimes this may be the case, but the reality is often the contrary. As followers of Christ, the seasons in which we bear an abundance of patience, joy, love, and other sweet fruit will often be the seasons of our most difficult circumstances. To take things one step further, could it be that our least fruitful seasons are the times when things seem to be going our way?

**COULD IT BE THAT OUR LEAST FRUITFUL SEASONS ARE THE TIMES WHEN THINGS SEEM TO BE GOING OUR WAY?**

Are there situations you are trying to avoid or escape where God is telling you, "I want you to bear fruit so those around you can taste it"? What fruit are you tasting and enjoying from the lives of godly people around you? Could it be that hardship in their lives is working to bring about this beautiful result? Hebrews 12:11, speaking of God's children, says, *"For the moment all discipline seems painful rather than pleasant, but later it yields the peaceful fruit of righteousness to those who have been trained by it."*

When we meditate on the Word day and night and simply respond to it in obedience in our own lives, we will bear fruit in season, as a tree planted by streams of water. This is, literally, our calling. In John 15:16, Jesus says, *"You did not choose Me, but I chose you and appointed you that you should go and bear fruit and that your fruit should abide* [or remain].*"*

**SELF-EXAMINATION:** The blessed man is a source of provision to a hurting world, and he will yield fruit. What fruit is the world tasting from your life today? Who is picking this fruit? In what areas is the Master Gardener pruning your life so that you might bear more fruit? Remember, your fruit-bearing will not be self-serving. Its purpose will be to serve others so that, through you, they might taste and see that God is good. Are you discouraged, feeling that you are being used by others? Rejoice that God has chosen to work through a fragile and broken vessel like you. We are the light of the world (Matthew 5:14). Our calling is to bear fruit, not to produce it, and that begins by our responding positively to His Word in our lives.

A TIME FOR

*Reflection*

> Brightly beams our Father's mercy
> From His lighthouse evermore,
> But to us He gives the keeping of
> The lights along the shore.
> Dark the night of sin has settled;
> Loud the angry billows roar;
> Eager eyes are watching, longing,
> For the lights along the shore.
> Let the lower lights be burning,
> Send a gleam across the wave.
> Some poor fainting, struggling seaman,
> You may rescue, you may save.[30]

**QUESTIONS TO CONSIDER: Before addressing these questions, take a few minutes to write down your initial thoughts and reactions to this chapter. What stands out to you? What questions come to mind? What does your flesh initially want to resist?**

1. What fruit (of the Spirit) are you benefiting from and/or enjoying in others right now? What circumstances are they walking through in order to bear such fruit?

2. What is the difference between bearing fruit and producing fruit? How might you be trying to produce results in your life rather than responding to the circumstances God has entrusted to you?

3. What current situations in your life (be specific) are an opportunity to bear fruit for the benefit of others?

4. What fruit (wholesome or harmful) are people picking from your life? Does the fruit of your life point them to Jesus or to the world?

5. Who do you think is currently enjoying the fruit in your life? Is there a way in which you could make the fruit more accessible to others?

6. How might God want to thin your fruit (expose you to those who can pick the fruit)? Why is thinning necessary if we are to bear more fruit?

7. In what ways are you perhaps more focused on the fruit itself rather than on seeing fruit as a direct result of knowing God and His Word?

# Notes

# THE *Patience* OF THE BLESSED MAN

**PSALM 1:1-3**   *Blessed is the man who walks not in the counsel of the wicked, nor stands in the way of sinners, nor sits in the seat of scoffers; but his delight is in the law of the Lord, and on His law he meditates day and night. He is like a tree planted by streams of water that yields its fruit **in its season**, and its leaf does not wither. In all that he does, he prospers.*

**BIG IDEA:**

THE **PATIENCE** OF THE BLESSED MAN BRINGS A CONTENTMENT TO HIS PRESENT SEASON AS HE WAITS EXPECTANTLY ON THE LORD TO FULLY ACCOMPLISH HIS DESIGN FOR THIS PHASE OF LIFE.

*T*here is a word...

We don't tend to excel at living it out, but we quickly notice when others don't extend it to us. It's one component of the fruit of the Spirit, and it comes appropriately in line following our discussions about the pain and the provision of the blessed man. Why now? According to James 1:3, testing creates an opportune context for the display of this necessary element of Christlikeness in our lives.

What is this marvelous quality that we so want to see exemplified in others but rarely wish for the opportunity to practice ourselves? You've likely already anticipated the answer (considering our title). Yes, it is patience. The **patience** of the blessed man.

Where is this patience of the blessed man found in Psalm 1? Look again at verse 3: *"He is like a tree planted by streams of water that yields its fruit in its season."* The phrase *"in its season"* provides our answer. The psalmist speaks of seasonal fruit. This is telling. **There is a sense in which the blessed man is not yielding all fruit all the time.** Today, many western grocery stores import extensively, allowing one to purchase their favorite fruit year-round (albeit at drastically elevated prices). This was not the case in Senegal where I grew up. When something was in season, you could buy it. When it wasn't, you were out of luck.

But look at this psalm.

A tree bears its fruit in its intended season. This is exciting. For example, patience is a fruit of the Spirit, so there will be a season in my life when I will bear patience.

**A TREE BEARS ITS FRUIT IN ITS INTENDED SEASON.**

Don't misunderstand. Patience is always the right response for a believer in Christ Jesus, but it will not always be on vivid display in my life. There will be seasons for patience. Understand also that the season which results in our bearing a certain fruit will tend to be a season of difficulty. An abundance of fruit will not normally grow during easy times. If we ignore this spiritual reality, we may try to avoid, or even plead with our heavenly Father to remove, the very season designed by Him to bring forth the greatest yield.

**AN ABUNDANCE OF FRUIT WILL NOT NORMALLY GROW DURING EASY TIMES.**

Consider the example of waiting on God for a spouse.

I was well over thirty years old before I married. Having stood as the Best Man in five weddings, a groomsman many times, and even having performed several wedding ceremonies, I must admit, the thought entered my mind, "Will I ever stand as a groom on the wedding stage?" But it was in that beautiful phase of life that God taught me that He had laid before me some unique opportunities to bear fruit for the benefit of others, fruit that would not have come through the circumstances of marriage. His desire was not that I should "wait for marriage." He was asking me to worship and faithfully serve Him in His particular calling to me at that time. He changed my heart and allowed me to treasure and use those years of singleness to pour out my life for Him in unique ways. Now, as a husband and father, the opportunities are still great, but they have changed. The lesson? **Don't rush into the next season; rather, ask the Lord to fully use this particular season to bear fruit for His glory.**

> **I MUST ADMIT, THE THOUGHT ENTERED MY MIND, "WILL I EVER STAND AS A GROOM ON THE WEDDING STAGE?"**

It's important that we clearly see the picture the psalmist has painted.

**We often pray for a fruitful life, but do we then try to pray away every opportunity the Lord brings into our lives which will bring forth the desired fruit?** Patience is best displayed against a dark backdrop of pressure, disappointment, rudeness, or irritation. We might wish for a season to come or, contrariwise, for a season to end, but, my friends, seasons will come and seasons will go—*all in His time.*

How easy it is to live life short-sighted. I could certainly pray right now, "Lord, please remove this cancer from my life!" But I'd do well to ask a few questions first.

- What if God is using cancer to reveal patience, trust, and joy in the midst of trials?

- What if cancer is the conduit through which He wishes to demonstrate His peace?

- What if God is using cancer to draw souls to want to know Him more?

- Would I seriously want Him to remove my cancer at such a high cost?

I find myself praying often, "Lord, please don't remove my cancer until You have fully received the glory You desire from this test." There are seasons. Praise God when it's fruit-bearing season.

If you're in the midst of a tough season right now, be encouraged; it *will* pass. In cancer, I have had to fully recognize this: Whether through physical healing or through eternal healing, *it will pass*; this is not the last chapter for the child of God. **When you don't see certain fruit in your life, the right response and only solution is to continue digging your roots deep into the Word of God.** And, as you continually respond to the law of the Lord, be prepared, because the season for bearing fruit *is* coming.

Maybe you *feel* that your life is always *"out of season"* and you feel dry. Or perhaps you sense that your life is always *"in season"* and you feel overwhelmed. Keep in mind that a tree is heaviest when it is *bearing* fruit. It's easy to confuse **fruit-bearing** with **fatigue**.

Perhaps you are asking, "God, can I have a break from this season?"

There is **good news**.

You *can't* produce fruit. That is not your responsibility. Your responsibility is simply to *bear* fruit. In season and out of season, the Bible reminds us that our love-response to God is to *"keep His commands"* (John 15:14). Earlier in that chapter we are told, *"Abide in Me, and I in you. As the branch cannot bear fruit by itself, unless it abides in the vine, neither can you, unless you abide in Me. I am the vine; you are the branches. Whoever abides in Me and I in him, he it is that bears much fruit, for apart from Me you can do nothing"* (John 15:4-5).

> **YOU CAN'T PRODUCE FRUIT. THAT IS NOT YOUR RESPONSIBILITY. YOUR RESPONSIBILITY IS SIMPLY TO BEAR FRUIT.**

TURN THE PAGE
FOR A TIME OF
*Reflection*

**SELF-EXAMINATION:** What step of simple obedience would God have you take today? Perhaps this step will be an attitude check, an act of service, a change of schedule, a simple confession, or renewed priorities. Are you discouraged by the season in which you find yourself? Are you longing for a different season and thereby missing the opportunities of this season? You have the opportunity to bear fruit today, even if it's not the fruit you were wanting to bear. Seasons come and seasons go, but every season is an opportunity to know Him and, ultimately, to bear wholesome fruit so the world might see Christ in you, the hope of glory (Colossians 1:27). Keep in mind that this is a work which the Lord has begun in us, and He will finish it.

A TIME FOR

*Reflection*

> *Finish, then, Thy new creation;*
> *Pure and spotless, let us be.*
> *Let us see Thy great salvation,*
> *Perfectly restored in Thee.*
> *Changed from glory into glory*
> *Till in heaven we take our place,*
> *Till we cast our crowns before Thee,*
> *Lost in wonder, love, and praise.*[31]

**QUESTIONS TO CONSIDER:** Before addressing these questions, take a few minutes to write down your initial thoughts and reactions to this chapter. What stands out to you? What questions come to mind? What does your flesh initially want to resist?

1. What fruit is "in season" in your life? Consider the fruit (think of Galatians 5:22-23) God is producing in your life. What are the circumstances surrounding that fruit?

2. Describe a situation where others showed great patience with you and allowed you to taste their fruit? How would you have felt if they had refused to bear fruit during that season?

3. Is there something that you are trying to pray away, something that God intends to use?

4. Is there a season you have been waiting for which doesn't seem to be coming? How is that waiting pictured in this psalm? What is God bearing in and through you in the waiting?

5. Give some past examples of circumstances where the fruit of patience was bred.

6. In what circumstances of today is God teaching you patience? How are you responding to these circumstances? Is it, "Lord, please don't remove or change (insert situation here) until You have fully received the glory," or are you complaining and wishing for circumstances to change as quickly as possible?

7. What simple step of obedience can I take today? How can I be accountable to following through on the simple step God is leading me to take?

# Notes

# THE *Permission* OF THE BLESSED MAN

**PSALM 1:1-3** *Blessed is the man who walks not in the counsel of the wicked, nor stands in the way of sinners, nor sits in the seat of scoffers; but his delight is in the law of the Lord, and on His law he meditates day and night. He is like a tree planted by streams of water that* **yields** *its fruit in its season, and its leaf does not wither. In all that he does, he prospers.*

**BIG IDEA:**

WE ARE TO **PERMISSIVELY** YIELD TO GOD'S PERFECT WORK IN OUR LIFE BY SURRENDERING OUR WILL TO THE WORD OF GOD.

The woman or man who doesn't live the blessed life (according to Psalm 1) is one who values the world more than the Word and who settles for mediocrity rather than savoring the riches of meditation. (Again, this statement is not intended to condemn but to encourage us all in a choice we have been given.)

Look at the word in Psalm 1:3 translated as *yields*: *"He is like a tree planted by streams of water that* **yields** *its fruit in its season."* Now let's look at the **permission** of the blessed man. In Hebrew, the word for *yields* is *nathan*. I did a double-take on this one since Nathan is my given name.

This word *nathan* can mean "to give, grant, deliver, or yield." It's the giving of a gift by the object of the sentence. Here, the tree is the giver, and it is giving, granting, delivering, the gift of fruit. Think in terms of a package delivery service. They don't design or produce the item; they only deliver it to the recipient.

It's vital that we notice the *permission* aspect of fruit-bearing. Permission must in some way be granted in order for that fruit to be allowed to grow. Remember when Jesus invited his disciples to follow Him in Matthew 16:24? He clearly told them, *"If anyone would come after Me, **let** him deny himself and take up his cross and follow Me." "Let him..."* Following Christ involves a choice. Taking up your cross doesn't happen by accident. There is no "Oops, I have a cross. Where did that come from?" There is intentionality. Paul exhorted the Philippians to, *"**Let** this mind be in you which was also in Christ Jesus"* (Philippians 2:5 NKJV). Literally, choose to think like Jesus Christ.

**TAKING UP YOUR CROSS DOESN'T HAPPEN BY ACCIDENT. THERE IS INTENTIONALITY.**

Neither following Jesus nor thinking like Jesus happen by accident. They are each the result of intentionally meditating on the law of the Lord day and night. It is then, and only then, that our life will be like a tree planted by streams of water. It is then that we will begin to recognize the value of eternal things in everyday life.

But there is another angle.

Gravity is a fact of planet earth. Imagine if I were to hold up a ball and say, "I'm going to drop this. Let it fall." The ball is going to fall to the ground unless someone stops it. Constant meditation on God's Word is like gravity. It just happens. It does what it does. For those in Christ, He is *for* us, and He *wants* to work in us. He wants to work in you and He wants to work in me *more* than we want Him to work in us. His desire is that you would bear much fruit. Like gravity, *let* it happen; *let* Him do His work. *"Let the word of Christ dwell in you richly, teaching and admonishing one another in all wisdom, singing psalms and hymns and spiritual songs, with thankfulness in your hearts to God"* (Colossians 3:16).

Are we willing to yield fruit? For this to occur, we must be willing to surrender to the One who is able and willing to produce fruit. And surrendering to the One who produces fruit requires surrendering to the practice of meditating on His Word. By meditating on other things, we can nonchalantly or unknowingly allow the things of the world to capture our hearts and our minds, thereby obstructing or intercepting what the Spirit of God wants to do in our life through His Word. In what area of our lives are we refusing to yield to God's Word?

> **BY MEDITATING ON OTHER THINGS, WE CAN NONCHALANTLY OR UNKNOWINGLY ALLOW THE THINGS OF THE WORLD TO CAPTURE OUR HEARTS AND OUR MINDS.**

Previously we discussed the word *yield* in the context of traffic signs. To yield the right of way doesn't mean we can't proceed, but it does mean that someone else has the priority and that we must allow them to proceed before us. So it is with bearing fruit. We will be fruitful only as a result of yielding the right-of-way to the Word of God. Are you yielding to the Word and the work of God in your life?

TURN THE PAGE
FOR A TIME OF
*Reflection*

**SELF-EXAMINATION:** Consider what or where you might be refusing to yield. An attitude? Forgiveness toward someone? Control over something? Perhaps your unwillingness manifests itself in complaining, worry, or bitterness. What is it that God wants you to give or give up or yield to Him today? As we look into His Word and yield to Him who is the Word, we will bear much fruit, and we will be *"like a tree planted by streams of water that yields its fruit in its season"* (Psalm 1:3). Yield to the Word, and He will do what only He can do: bring forth fruit in our lives.

A TIME FOR

*Reflection*

> Oh, we never can know what the Lord will bestow
> Of the blessings for which we have prayed,
> Till our body and soul He doth fully control,
> And our all on the altar is laid.
> Who can tell all the love He will send from above,
> And how happy our hearts will be made;
> Of the fellowship sweet, we shall share at His feet,
> When our all on the altar is laid.
> Is your all on the altar of sacrifice laid?
> Your heart, does the Spirit control?
> You can only be blest, and have peace and sweet rest,
> As you yield Him your body and soul.[32]

**QUESTIONS TO CONSIDER: Before addressing these questions, take a few minutes to write down your initial thoughts and reactions to this chapter. What stands out to you? What questions come to mind? What does your flesh initially want to resist?**

1. When you hear the word *yield*, what thoughts come to your mind (weakness, submission, etc.)?

2. We yield to things and people every day (vehicles, bosses, desires, etc.). Take inventory, listing at least five areas in which you yield on a daily basis.

3. Choose one thing/person you yield to, and examine how that sphere of your life would look if you first yielded fully to God's Word in that area.

4. What area of life are you intentionally not yielding to Christ? Be honest. Let God examine your heart in this matter.

5. What keeps you from yielding *to the meditation* of God's Word? (The question is not "What keeps you from yielding to God's Word?")

6. How might you make an active choice to *"take up* [the] *cross"* today? What would that look like in various areas of your life: thoughts, words, plans, actions, etc.?

7. What biblical character, other than Jesus Christ, do you consider an example of one who was wholly yielded to God? Give a specific example from their life.

# Notes

# THE *Procreation* OF THE BLESSED MAN

**PSALM 1:1-3** *Blessed is the man who walks not in the counsel of the wicked, nor stands in the way of sinners, nor sits in the seat of scoffers; but his delight is in the law of the Lord, and on His law he meditates day and night. He is like a tree planted by streams of water **that yields its fruit** in its season, and its leaf does not wither. In all that he does, he prospers.*

**BIG IDEA:**

AS WE BEAR FRUIT FOR THE HUNGRY, THEY WILL SCATTER THE GOOD SEED ON NEW SOIL, RESULTING IN THE **PROCREATION** OF NEW TREES FOR THE LORD.

When I pick fruit from a tree, I can always be certain of one thing. Sure, the obvious occurs. The fruit is taken, consumed, and enjoyed. But what am I always sure to find? Take an avocado, for instance. **When I cut it open, I find a seed inside.** It's inevitable. After all, the definition of a fruit is "the sweet and fleshy product of a tree or other plant that contains seed and can be eaten as food." Without a seed, there is no fruit. Where there is fruit, there are seeds.

Fruit are seed-bearing structures which develop from the ovary of a flowering plant, whereas vegetables are all other plant parts, including roots, leaves, and stems. Even squash and tomatoes are technically fruit because they are the seed-bearers of the plants. We read of the beginnings of this great design of creation when God said, *"Let the earth sprout vegetation, plants yielding seed, and fruit trees bearing fruit in which is their seed, each according to its kind"* (Genesis 1:11). It is significant that Psalm 1 refers to fruit.

Why is this important?

Look again at Psalm 1:3. *"Like a tree planted by streams of water that yields its fruit."* The Creator of fruit and of life itself knew what He was talking about. The purpose of seeds is to reproduce, multiply, propagate. Reproduction. Procreation. And what is being produced in this verse? Fruit. And seeds. An avocado has one seed, but one tree can produce 200-300 avocados in a single season.

**THE PURPOSE OF SEEDS IS TO**
- **REPRODUCE**
- **MULTIPLY**
- **PROPAGATE.**

**REPRODUCTION. PROCREATION.**

Consider the implications. One seed, producing 200-300 avocados, each with its own seed, creates the potential to produce *hundreds of trees.* In the same way, we are to bear fruit. Much fruit. And as we dig our roots deep into the Word of God, we *will* bear fruit, the fruit of the Spirit, and in so doing, we procreate. Never underestimate the power of procreation.

But does the fruit, once it has been picked, end with the one who picked it? No. Generally, once it has been eaten, the seed is dropped elsewhere. Likewise, when the fruit of love or faithfulness or gentleness is picked from our life and is tasted and enjoyed by those around us, we can only imagine where those seeds might be disseminated. The one who has eaten the fruit may go on to share it with others so that they can also enjoy its sweetness. They share what

**DOES THE FRUIT, ONCE IT HAS BEEN PICKED, END WITH THE ONE WHO PICKED IT? NO.**

they have tasted, and so its impact multiplies. Other times, storm winds pick up the seed and carry it far beyond the reaches of the original tree. As this happens, some of those seeds take root and spring to life. Procreation.

The promise by Jesus is straightforward. *"I am the vine; you are the branches. Whoever abides in Me and I in him, he it is that bears much fruit, for apart from Me you can do nothing"* (John 15:5). You might ask yourself these questions: How can I make a difference in this world? How can I impact society? How can I truly impact my spouse, my kids, my family? How can I be a faithful witness of the gospel? The clear teaching of Jesus Christ to His disciples was that *"by this all people will know that you are My disciples, if you have love for one another"* (John 13:35-36). As we simply abide in the vine, soaking in the love of God toward us, **our reasonable response will be to share with others the love of Calvary that we have tasted.** It will be in tasting the fruit of God's love through us that the world will know and believe.

> **HOW CAN I MAKE A DIFFERENCE IN THIS WORLD?**
>
> **YOU [CAN] YIELD AND BEAR FRUIT AND DELIVER THAT FOOD TO THE HUNGRY.**

So, the result? You will yield and bear fruit and deliver that food to the hungry. Those looking for authenticity, life, and hope in a world of chaos and confusion will taste, through your life, the sweetness of *"Christ in you, the hope of glory"* (Colossians 1:27). And, having tasted this fruit, perhaps they will spread the good seed through their words—in their conversations or on their posts—thus planting it in other soils.

> **SOME SOIL WILL BE WELL PREPARED TO RECEIVE THE GOOD SEED AND WILL BEAR AN ABUNDANCE OF FRUIT: THIRTY-, SIXTY-, AND A HUNDRED-FOLD.**

Some by the wayside, sure. Some in rocky soil, yes. Some among thorns, of course. But some soil will be well prepared to receive the good seed and will bear an abundance of fruit: thirty-, sixty-, and a hundred-fold. This is the procreation of the blessed man!

At the wedding feast in Cana, Mary told the servants, *"Do whatever He tells you"* (John 2:5). That is how we are to respond to the Word of God.

Digging our roots down deep into it.
Making that Word the priority, the passion, and the preoccupation of our life.
Doing all that He tells us.
Immediately.
Fully.

Our purpose is to bear fruit. And when we do, the same may be said of us that was said of Peter and John in Acts 4:13: *And they recognized that **they had been with Jesus.*** The blessed man of Psalm 1 reproduces. His is a life with an enduring legacy.

**SELF-EXAMINATION:** Is that our story? Be honest. Where is the Holy Spirit stirring you up, making you uncomfortable? How are you responding to His conviction in your life? This journey is about responding to the Spirit of God's simple, daily, moment-by-moment conviction that comes from *"the sword of the Spirit, which is the word of God"* (Ephesians 6:17). Do you respond to the Word in your conversation? Do you respond to the Word when you're alone? Do you respond to the Word in your attitude? Do you respond to the Word in your responses to others? Do you respond to the Word in your posts? Do you respond to the Word in your thoughts? Do you respond to the Word in your prioritizing? Do you respond to the Word in your preaching? Do you respond to the Word in your love for others? May the seeds from the fruit of your life be scattered all around this hurting world, that all may see and taste for themselves the grace and goodness of our God.

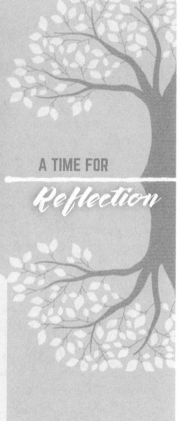

A TIME FOR

*Reflection*

> *Do we live so close to the Lord today,*
> *Passing to and fro on life's busy way,*
> *That the world in us can a likeness see to the Man of Calvary?*
> *Do we love, with love to His own akin,*
> *All His creatures lost in the mire of sin?*
> *Will we reach out a hand whatso'er it cost, to reclaim a sinner lost?*
> *As an open book they our lives will read,*
> *To our words and acts giving daily heed;*
> *Will they be attracted, or turn away from the Man of Calvary?*
> *Can the world see Jesus in me? Can the world see Jesus in you?* [33]

**QUESTIONS TO CONSIDER: Before addressing these questions, take a few minutes to write down your initial thoughts and reactions to this chapter. What stands out to you? What questions come to mind? What does your flesh initially want to resist?**

1. Think of a fruit you have tasted recently from the life of another. How was the seed of that fruit then disseminated from your life? Did you just drop it? Share it intentionally with another? Learn from it? Be specific.

2. Take time to journal about one person in your life whose seeds, though small, have spread mightily because of the sweetness of the fruit.

3. What fruit (good or bad) are others picking from your life? Where might those seeds be spreading?

4. Considering the responsibility of procreation, how does this lesson change the way you intentionally view your thoughts, words, and actions?

5. Think of an example of bad fruit that spread beyond the original tree. How is that a warning to you?

6. What seeds might you have spread from bad fruit which you have eaten that are now bearing bad fruit in others? How should you address this sin in your life?

7. What fruit would those who encounter you say they are tasting?

# Notes

# THE *Personalization* OF THE BLESSED MAN

**PSALM 1:1-3**    *Blessed is the man who walks not in the counsel of the wicked, nor stands in the way of sinners, nor sits in the seat of scoffers; but his delight is in the law of the Lord, and on His law he meditates day and night. He is like a tree planted by streams of water that yields **its fruit** in its season, and its leaf does not wither. In all that he does, he prospers.*

**BIG IDEA:**

GOD'S PLAN FOR YOU IS **PERSONALIZED.** HE CALLS YOU TO BEAR THE FRUIT OF *YOUR* TREE, TO BE FAITHFUL WHERE HE HAS PLANTED *YOU.*

The purpose of our journey into this psalm is not to focus on ourselves but is, rather, to help us understand God's desire for each of us to enjoy the blessed life He designed for His people. Notice God's **personalization** of the fruit that He produces and that we bear. *"He is like a tree planted by streams of water that yields its fruit"* (Psalm 1:3). *Personalization* can be defined as "the action of making something identifiable as belonging to a particular person." There is a personal aspect inherent in the blessed life. Notice the words, *"its fruit."* It does not simply say, "He is like a tree planted by streams of water that yields fruit," nor, "He is like a tree planted by streams of water that yields different fruit at different times," and not even, "He is like a tree planted by streams of water that yields 'Christian' fruit." Rather, this is very specific to the individual: *"He is like a tree planted by streams of water that yields **its** fruit."*

What an encouragement this is for each of us.

God doesn't call you to bear the fruit that someone else is bearing. It's easy to focus on the fruit that you're *not* bearing—by comparing yourself with your neighbor, spouse, church leader, or friend. It's easy to look at the ministry of others and to think of it as more effective, more dramatic, more fun, or more fruitful. But **the reality is that God has called you to bear the fruit of *your* tree. He calls you to be faithful in the place where He has planted *you*.**

> IT'S EASY TO FOCUS ON THE FRUIT THAT YOU'RE *NOT* BEARING— BY COMPARING YOURSELF WITH [OTHERS]. BUT GOD HAS CALLED YOU TO BEAR THE FRUIT OF *YOUR* TREE.

Peter reminds the church:

> *"As each has received a gift, use it to serve one another, as good stewards of God's varied grace: whoever speaks, as one who speaks oracles of God; whoever serves, as one who serves by the strength that God supplies—in order that in everything God may be glorified through Jesus Christ. To Him belong glory and dominion forever and ever. Amen"* (I Peter 4:10-11).

I vividly remember many afternoons of playing football (soccer) on the sandy streets of my neighborhood in Saint Louis, Senegal. We would spend hours under the hot sun, chasing our half-deflated ball around on the scalding Saharan sand (usually barefoot), but our game had a fundamental flaw. There was glory in scoring goals but little or no glory to be gained elsewhere on the playing field. Thus, most of the boys wanted to play forward, the position that usually scores. I was generally the goalkeeper, and it was frustratingly common for the defense to break down. We would give up easy goals all because everyone wanted to score and no one wanted to defend.

All too often the same rings true within the body of Christ.

According to 1 Corinthians 4:2, we are called to be faithful stewards, not stars. How easy it is to seek a place of prominence rather than a place that requires faith-fulness. But God doesn't call us to be famous. He calls us to be faithful.

**WE ARE CALLED TO BE FAITHFUL *STEWARDS*, NOT *STARS*.**

The prophet Elijah threw his mantle on Elisha, thereby marking Elisha's call by God. Elisha then spent the next fourteen to eighteen years ministering without a single mention of his name on the pages of Scripture. Those years are obscure to us; we're simply told that he *"assisted"* Elijah (1 Kings 19:21) and *"poured water on the hands of Elijah"* (2 Kings 3:11). This man, one of the greatest Old Testament prophets, left a successful and comfortable life in order to wholly follow the Lord. Obedience to God's call led him not to opulence but to obscurity. How many of us would have quit at some point during that decade and a half of humble and, at times, seemingly demeaning service?

**WHAT GETS IN THE WAY AND KEEPS YOU FROM BEARING THE FRUIT THAT THE LORD INTENDS FOR YOU TO BEAR?**

Allow me to ask, "What gets in the way and keeps you from bearing the fruit that the Lord intends for you to bear?" Do you allow your perception of value to impede your faithfulness to God's Word? I remember a conversation I had with one of my Arab peers when I was a young man working in the Middle East seeking to reach street children with the love of Christ. He suggested that there was value in serving the hurting, but then quickly added, "I don't want to waste my life like you."

Psalm 1:1 speaks of the man who listens to the counsel of the wicked. Expect the "counsellors" of this world to see your life as a waste.

They might suggest that what you're doing
doesn't have true value.

They might tell you that what you're doing
is below your pay grade.

They might flatter you by saying that what you're doing
is below your skill level and is an insult to your person.

Christ had a **drastically** different scale for measuring value and reward.

Jesus taught, *"Whoever receives you receives Me, and whoever receives Me receives Him who sent Me. The one who receives a prophet because he is a prophet will receive a prophet's reward, and the one who receives a righteous person because he is a righteous person will receive a righteous person's reward"* (Matthew 10:40-41).

Do you get this? Because if you *do*, this changes *everything*.

Welcome a servant of the Lord—you'll get a servant's reward. Serve a minister of the gospel—you'll be given a minister's reward. Labor fervently in prayer for those who are rescuing children from the brothels—you'll receive the same reward as they. Generously and sacrificially give and give of all that God has given you so that the gospel might reach the unreached peoples of the world—you will be given the same reward as those whose sandals are getting dirty! The Word is, *"**Whatever** you do, work heartily, as for the Lord and not for men"* (Colossians 3:23).

>We are a *team*.
>>We are a *body*.
>>>We are *the bride of Christ*.

This isn't a mere picture.
It's reality.

1 Corinthians 3:6-9 tells us, *"I planted, Apollos watered, but God gave the growth. So neither he who plants nor he who waters is anything, but only God who gives the growth. He who plants and he who waters are one, and each will receive his wages according to his labor. For we are God's fellow workers. You are God's field, God's building."* So, whoever you are and wherever you are, bear the fruit God wants to produce in you.

TURN THE PAGE
FOR A TIME OF
*Reflection*

**SELF-EXAMINATION:** Let's not be blinded by the distracting opinions of the wicked. The true questions are these: Are we being faithful to the Word that we meditate on day and night? Do our lives glorify God moment by moment? Is His glory our reward? Do we measure value by how many see our work or by our obedience to the Lord and to His Word? Remember, your calling is not to compete with others in the Church but to be joyfully faithful in the responsibility entrusted to you. It's about faithfulness to the Word, not fame before the world.

> We are the body of which the Lord is Head,
> Called to obey Him, now risen from the dead.
> He wills us be a family, diverse yet truly one.
> O let us give our gifts to God,
> And so shall His work on earth be done.[34]

**QUESTIONS TO CONSIDER: Before addressing these questions, take a few minutes to write down your initial thoughts and reactions to this chapter. What stands out to you? What questions come to mind? What does your flesh initially want to resist?**

1. Give an example where you've been tempted to envy someone else's gift or role in the body of Christ. Why were you (potentially) jealous?

2. How does jealousy keep you from seeing what God has for you?

3. Even if you don't say it or think you believe it, do you live and act as if God is more glorified by work or service for Him which is more visible and public? Explain.

4. Are there times when you grumble and complain (out loud or in your heart) about how God made you (personality type, appearance, interests) or about what God has called you to do (9-5 job, church role, serving others, etc.)?

5. Consider the body of Christ like a sports team in the Olympics. The assistant coach gets the same gold medal as the leading scorer. What parts of Christ's body have you previously deemed less valuable? Why? What would repentance look like in your life regarding this devaluation of your sister or brother?

6. From your current position, how might you serve another part of the body of Christ (fervent prayer, sacrificial giving, heartfelt encouragement, etc.)? Do you consider this service as less significant?

7. Do you actively view the body of Christ as your teammates? Make a chart of how you are working together with the rest of the body to accomplish His mission.

# Notes

## THE *Present* OF THE BLESSED MAN

**PSALM 1:1-3**    *Blessed is the man who walks not in the counsel of the wicked, nor stands in the way of sinners, nor sits in the seat of scoffers; but his delight is in the law of the Lord, and on His law he meditates day and night. He is like a tree planted by streams of water **that yields its fruit** in its season, and its leaf does not wither. In all that he does, he prospers.*

**BIG IDEA:**

MEDITATING ON THE WORD OF GOD EQUIPS AND ENABLES US TO GIVE THOSE AROUND OUR LIVES A **PRESENT** THAT THEY CAN TASTE AND THEREBY ENJOY THE GOODNESS OF GOD.

*E*arlier in our expedition into Psalm 1, we looked at the word *yield (nathan)* and noticed that it requires a granting of permission, a delivering, and a giving, as we surrender to the Spirit's work in us. Let's now take a step beyond *permission* to look at the **present** of the blessed man. He first *presents* himself, then, additionally, he offers a *present*, just as you would put under a Christmas tree, take to a birthday party, or give to a loved one at any time as an expression of love.

**What is this "present", this gift, and where is it found in these verses?**

Notice the action that takes place. The blessed man *chooses* to meditate on the law of the Lord day and night (Psalm 1:2). And the reason he does so is that others might enjoy the blessings of this fruit. Just as we saw his *provision* (fruit) and *permission* (yielding), so too we now see the man of Psalm 1 meditating on the law of the Lord—not just so he can be blessed, but because he knows that it is also the way to bless the world—and in this we find the *present* of the blessed man.

When you awake in the morning, you might prefer to stay in your warm bed and push the snooze button more than a couple of times. Most likely, you're *not* thinking, "I really need to get up because there are souls that need to be influenced by seeing Christ in me today." Or, maybe you *do* have this early-morning perspective!

Whatever your "present" case, this is a present you can choose to offer daily to a hurting and desperate world.

It isn't easy to meditate on the law of the Lord *day and night,* and any person who suggests that it is, isn't doing it. Yes, this pursuit of sweetness and intimacy with the Lord Himself is an absolute pleasure, but it is *not* easy. You cannot simply set your mind and heart to auto-pilot and expect them to fly straight on their own. It requires discipline. And that is why it is helpful to be reminded of the big picture, that our pursuit to know and enjoy God intimately is not *only* for us; it is also our necessary preparation if we are to share God's glory and gospel with those around us and beyond—even throughout the whole earth.

> **INTIMACY WITH THE LORD HIMSELF IS AN ABSOLUTE PLEASURE, BUT IT IS *NOT* EASY.**

**But this gets serious. *Very* serious.** Do I understand the value of bearing fruit and its interconnectedness with every aspect of my life? Consider this: If I truly love my wife, I'll be meditating on the law of the Lord day and night. If I truly love my kids,

I'll desire to filter everything through God's Word. If I desire for the gospel to be clearly seen in me and around me, I will be feeding my soul on the wholesome Scriptures which nourish and equip me. Why? Only meditating on the Word of God teaches me and refines me and enables me to bear the fruit that my wife, my children, and others will taste *and truly enjoy*. This is my gift to others.

**ONLY MEDITATING ON THE WORD OF GOD ENABLES ME TO BEAR THE FRUIT THAT OTHERS WILL TASTE AND TRULY ENJOY. THIS IS MY GIFT TO OTHERS.**

Meditating on God's Word day and night doesn't mean disconnecting from the world. Rather, it means viewing every element of our day through the lens of God's heart and not becoming distracted by society's labels which seek to demean, devalue, and divide souls for whom Christ died. It is reminding ourselves daily of the grace, love, forgiveness, and peace that we have tasted at Calvary so that our spouse, kids, and coworkers can taste the same. It is catching a fresh glimpse of God's eternal plan so that, instead of being overwhelmed by the burdens of today, our eyes are opened to the spiritual battle taking place around us.

Even Jesus Christ said, *"I do as the Father has commanded Me, so that the world may know that I love the Father"* (John 14:31). Why is this so important? The world, your friends, and even your family don't need to see you. They need to see Christ *in* you. Do not misunderstand. Our heart should be focused *primarily* on personally knowing Christ, but we are also called to love others as God does. And the only way we can do this successfully is by allowing the heart of God to control every aspect of our life. What is the genesis of such a journey? Meditating day and night on the Word of God.

**THE WORLD, YOUR FRIENDS, AND EVEN YOUR FAMILY DON'T NEED TO SEE *YOU*. THEY NEED TO SEE *CHRIST IN YOU*.**

**SELF-EXAMINATION:** If we know the end result, that the one who thinks on the law of the Lord day and night will be blessed and will bear fruit, and if we believe that God's Word is true, what is holding us back in this most worthy pursuit? Could it be that we are unaware of the impact our personal life has on the lives of others? Could it be that we don't really believe this to be the blessed life? Could it be that we are actually so selfish that we don't care about those around us? Do we doubt that true blessedness comes from keeping God's Word in our minds and hearts day and night?

A TIME FOR

*Reflection*

Oh Jesus Christ, grow Thou in me, and all things else recede;
My heart be daily nearer Thee, from sin be daily freed.
In Thy bright beams which on me fall, fade every evil thought;
That I am nothing, Thou art all, I would be daily taught.
More of Thy glory, let me see, Thou Holy, Wise, and True;
I would Thy living image be, in joy and sorrow too.
Fill me with gladness from above, hold me by strength divine;
Lord, let the glow of Thy great love through all my being shine.
Make this poor self grow less and less, be Thou my life and aim;
Oh, make me daily, through Thy grace, more meet to bear Thy Name.[35]

**QUESTIONS TO CONSIDER: Before addressing these questions, take a few minutes to write down your initial thoughts and reactions to this chapter. What stands out to you? What questions come to mind? What does your flesh initially want to resist?**

1. What present does your life offer to the needy world around you?

2. How are you intentionally living your private life so that others are free to pick the fruit of your spiritual investment?

3. How might you be more intentional in your study of the Word so that you are prepared to face your day and to offer the world a different attitude, perspective, and example? Take a few minutes to journal your thoughts.

4. How does meditation on God's Word affect the other presents you might offer to the world (evangelism, hospitality, etc.)?

5. In what ways might you be selfish with your life's disciplines, and how might this impact others around you?

6. What does meditating on God's Word day and night look like practically? Everyone's schedules are different, so tailor this question to your personal life.

7. Who is the first person that comes to mind, that you know personally, who gives a present to the world around them as a direct result of the time they spend with the Lord? How do they communicate this gift? I encourage you to thank them for the impact they have had in your life.

# Notes

## THE *Process* OF THE BLESSED MAN

**PSALM 1:1-3**   *Blessed is the man who walks not in the counsel of the wicked, nor stands in the way of sinners, nor sits in the seat of scoffers; but his delight is in the law of the Lord, and on His law he meditates day and night. He is like a tree planted by streams of water that **yields its fruit in its season**, and its leaf does not wither. In all that he does, he prospers.*

**BIG IDEA:**

AS WE GO THROUGH THE **PROCESS** REQUIRED TO BEAR FRUIT, WE MUST WAIT EXPECTANTLY FOR THE HARVEST WHICH IS SURE TO COME.

Once again, Psalm 1 brings a reality into the light: The blessed life is a **process**. The life of a seed is a journey. The text says, *"He is like a tree planted by streams of water that yields its fruit **in its season"*** (Psalm 1:3).

Recalling our discussion about fruit, we underlined the fact that every fruit has a seed, or seeds, which equips it to reproduce. Likewise, as we meditate on the Word of God, our lives bring forth spiritual fruit, which blesses others, which blesses others, and so on, and so on... The seeds by which we bless others have the potential to spread far and wide. But each seed must undergo a process. And, if we aren't careful, we will forget about that process and might adopt a mindset that will disillusion and discourage us.

So we need to reflect on the *process* involved in blessing.

When we know the way God works (as detailed in His Word), we are not shocked when He does precisely what He says He will do. In the natural realm, a field doesn't bear fruit in the same season in which the seed is planted. Planting and harvesting are not simultaneous. This was certainly obvious to me growing up around the peanut and millet fields of Senegal. People prepared the field, planted the seed, prayed for rain, and waited *months and months* for full growth.

**IN THE NATURAL REALM, A FIELD DOESN'T BEAR FRUIT IN THE SAME SEASON IN WHICH THE SEED IS PLANTED.**

So it is in the spiritual realm.

Though clearly speaking of the coming of the Lord, James presents us with a sure life principle in James 5:7. *"See how the farmer waits for the precious fruit of the earth, being patient about it, until it receives the early and the late rains."* As we go through the process required to bear the fruit of the Spirit, we can't expect the results to be immediately visible. But rest assured that God is at work. He is planting the seed, fertilizing and watering the soil, cultivating and pruning the young tree—until, ultimately, He will bring forth the fruit that He Himself has planned.

**WE CAN'T EXPECT THE RESULTS TO BE IMMEDIATELY VISIBLE. BUT REST ASSURED THAT GOD IS AT WORK.**

In short, the Psalm 1 process begins with meditation on the Word, pictured by the tree planted by streams of water, and, after a period of watering, feeding, and growing, finally yields its fruit in its season. The parallel is reflected in 1 Corinthians 3:6 where Paul says, *"I planted, Apollos watered, but God gave the increase"* (NKJV).

The word *process*, defined as "a series of steps taken in order to achieve a particular end," can sound like a long, drawn-out procedure, bringing discouragement and defeat. Yet, the process of this blessed man will eventually result not merely in his bearing fruit, but also in the dissemination of seeds and, eventually, in the multiplication of trees planted by the water—but all *in its season.* Psalm 145:15 affirms this (see also Psalm 104:27): *"The eyes of all look to You, and You give them their food in due season."*

> **Maybe you're discouraged with what you're seeing in this season of your life.**

Maybe it concerns your kids or a friend or a colleague. You've been faithfully investing and pouring into them, sharing Christ with them, loving them in countless ways, but nothing substantial seems to be happening. Maybe it concerns someone you long to see saved, or maybe it's a relationship in which you long for restoration and forgiveness. You see no fruit from your labor—at least not according to your definition. My friend, allow this reminder to permeate your heart. You have been called to bear fruit, not to produce it in another. Again, the good news is that God is at work. *"And let us not grow weary of doing good, for in due season we will reap, if we do not give up"* (Galatians 6:9).

**YOU HAVE BEEN CALLED TO *BEAR FRUIT*, NOT TO *PRODUCE IT IN ANOTHER.***

Harvesting does not come in the same season in which the seed is sown. As Ecclesiastes 3:1-8 reminds us, *"For everything there is a season and a time..."*

When a seed is planted, there is more than just delay; there is death. The seed goes into the ground, and there, alone in that dark chamber, cold and unseen by human eyes—there is a death, and a new life begins. As Jesus says in John 12:24-25, *"Truly, truly I say to you, unless a grain of wheat falls into the earth and dies, it remains alone; but if it dies, it bears much fruit. Whoever loves his life loses it, and whoever hates his life in this world will keep it for eternal life."*

I love this great promise from Isaiah 40:28-31. For a fresh hearing, let's read it from *The Message*:

> *Don't you know anything? Haven't you been listening? God doesn't come and go. God lasts. He's Creator of all you can see or imagine. He doesn't get tired out, doesn't pause to catch His breath. And He knows everything, inside and out. He energizes those who get tired, gives fresh strength to dropouts. For even young people tire and drop out, young folk in their prime stumble and fall. But those who wait upon God get fresh strength. They spread their wings and soar like eagles, they run and don't get tired, they walk and don't lag behind.*

**Waiting on God isn't so much like waiting in a doctor's office. It's more like being a server in a restaurant and faithfully waiting on a table. It is a purposeful and active waiting rather than a passive and aimless waiting.** The seed is planted, and so we wait—patiently, actively, expectantly. How? We constantly meditate on His Word and consistently obey it.

**SELF-EXAMINATION:** Are you looking for a quick product when God's plan is a well-thought-out process? Are you focused on some desired result when God's desire is a surrendered servant? My friend, are you waiting on the Lord? Psalm 130:5-6 tells us, *"I wait for the Lord, my soul does wait, and in His Word do I hope. My soul waits for the Lord more than the watchmen for the morning. Indeed, more than the watchmen for the morning"* (NASB). Are you waiting and doing nothing (like passively waiting in a doctor's office), or are you looking for every opportunity to more fully know and live out God's heart for your life (like actively serving in a restaurant) while you wait? Wait expectantly while serving faithfully. You are part of a grand story in which God wants to use you today while He continues to work in you. His process is perfect and will surely produce His desired product.

> *For the fruit of all creation, thanks be to God.*
> *For the gifts of every nation, thanks be to God.*
> *For the plowing, sowing, reaping,*
> *Silent growth while we are sleeping,*
> *Future needs in earth's safe keeping, thanks be to God.*[36]

**QUESTIONS TO CONSIDER: Before addressing these questions, take a few minutes to write down your initial thoughts and reactions to this chapter. What stands out to you? What questions come to mind? What does your flesh initially want to resist?**

1. Where are you wanting only the product, when God wants to use the process? (For example, you only want to be healed, but God wants to work in you and use you in the waiting.)

2. Give an example from your life where the process seemed to drag on and on. What did that process teach you?

3. What makes waiting difficult for you?

4. In what areas of your life are you waiting on God right now? Make a list. Now, go through that list, and try to determine if you are passively waiting or actively waiting.

5. What feelings tend to arise in "the process" when you're exhausted, disillusioned, and ready to quit? How might a view of the big picture change your perspective?

6. Think of those around you. How can you encourage others who have planted seeds and are now waiting for a fruitful season?

7. Give an example from Scripture where someone had to actively wait for God to work out their situation. What fruit came from that interim period that they may have chosen to avoid?

Notes

# THE *Promise* OF THE BLESSED MAN

**PSALM 1:1-3**   *Blessed is the man who walks not in the counsel of the wicked, nor stands in the way of sinners, nor sits in the seat of scoffers; but his delight is in the law of the Lord, and on His law he meditates day and night. He is like a tree planted by streams of water **that yields its fruit in its season**, and its leaf does not wither. In all that he does, he prospers.*

**BIG IDEA:**

THE BLESSED MAN TRUSTS THE **PROMISES** OF THE EVER-FAITHFUL ONE WHO DESIRES TO PRESERVE AND ETERNALLY PROSPER US.

From children's playgrounds to corporate offices, a word is thrown around which is intended to guarantee solemn commitment and bring about definite change. This word, and all its intentions, is commonly sealed by children with a pinky finger and in businesses with a pen. Sadly, all too often, the only change it brings is deep disappointment, severed friendships, and permanently broken relationships.

The word is **promise**.

The English word *promise* comes from the Latin words meaning "to send" and "forward." Tragically, the concept of a promise has lost much of its significance and value due to the failure of so many to keep their promises. But in Psalm 1, it is God sending forth the word, and *His* word we can trust and bank on. His promise is this: The one who *"meditates day and night" "in the law of the Lord"* will *"yield its fruit in its season."*

We must consider two factors of vital importance when determining the trustworthiness of any promise: (1) the one who is making the promise, and (2) the content of the promise itself. If the one making the promise is not trustworthy, the promise is worth little or nothing and opens the door for false expectations and sure disappointment. On the other hand, if the promise itself is worthless or useless, then it matters little who made the promise.

For now, let's focus on *the idea of a promise.*

In the *Journal of Business Ethics,* I saw an article that concluded, "Promise-keeping consistently was found to rank last in a hierarchy of workplace values."[37] Why? The promises being made could not be counted on. We live in a society, in a world, in political systems, and even, at times, in a church (sadly) where an individual's promise often means little. Simply consider the startling and tragic statistics of broken marriages. These reveal that divorce is often seen as an option from the start, even before the vows are spoken—vows, remember, which are taken *in the sight of God and in the presence of many witnesses.*

**"PROMISE-KEEPING CONSISTENTLY WAS FOUND TO RANK LAST IN A HIERARCHY OF WORKPLACE VALUES."**

**BUT THINGS ARE DRASTICALLY DIFFERENT WHEN GOD SPEAKS.**

But things are drastically different when God speaks. Indeed, *"all the promises of God find their Yes in Him"* (2 Corinthians 1:20). A powerful truth is presented in Hebrews 6:18. *"So that by two unchangeable things, in which it is impossible for God to lie, we who have fled for refuge might have strong encouragement to hold fast to the hope set before us."* I'm not sure whose promises you're trusting in today, but if your hope is resting in the promise of any human being— whether it be a husband, wife, parent, child, friend, or politician—or is placed in any product of human contrivance—church membership, business contract, bank statement, clean bill of health, retirement plan, or insurance policy—I can understand why you might be unsure, anxious, discouraged, or fearful. Promises made by mankind don't bring true peace, only conditional peace, because both mankind and human conditions change. But the promise in Psalm 1:3 is made by the unchangeable God. So if you, as His child, meditate on His Word day and night, your life *will* yield its fruit in its season.

**PROMISES MADE BY MANKIND DON'T BRING TRUE PEACE, ONLY CONDITIONAL PEACE.**

Here's a good question to ask yourself: Is my life spiritually healthy? This is really a two-part question. The first question is: (1) Am I in the Word of God, meditating on that Word throughout the day? Is His Word the filter for my thoughts and decisions? The second question is: (2) Am I *actually* surrendering to the Word of God in my priorities and choices? Is the Word of God my **true authority**? Or is it just a **good idea**?

When you can honestly answer "Yes" to those two elements and know them to be the realities of your life, you won't insist on understanding why things are the way they are, nor will you feel the need to calculate the value of the fruit you see (or *don't* see) in your life. Instead, your life will give evidence of the two characteristics of prospering which we read of in Psalm 1: You will be a tree whose leaves do not wither, and you will prosper in all that you do (Psalm 1:3). The promises God makes are always for our good. He wants to preserve us and prosper us in the eternal sense of these words. The specific day-to-day details of our lives may not always give clear evidence of this, but we can trust our God to guide us and to bless us each step of the way.

As a kid, I knew that my parents were for me and that they loved me. If they told me there was a special surprise that I would love, I didn't have to wonder whether or not it was good. I knew their heart for me. Simply put, I trusted the character of the ones making the promise rather than trusting in my comprehension of the promise itself.

> I TRUSTED THE CHARACTER OF THE ONES MAKING THE PROMISE RATHER THAN MY COMPREHENSION OF THE PROMISE ITSELF.

Do you trust God?

We are reminded in Romans 8:32, *"He who did not spare His own Son but gave Him up for us all, how will He not also with Him graciously give us all things?"* **The next time you are tempted to doubt God's care or compassion, look at the cross.** The next time you begin to doubt God's sincerity, consider the sufferings of His Son who willingly took on Himself the punishment for your sin and shame. *"For you know the grace of our Lord Jesus Christ, that though He was rich, yet for your sake He became poor, so that you by His poverty might become rich"* (2 Corinthians 8:9). But don't miss this detail. There's nothing here that says you'll *feel* like you're prospering. There's nothing that says others are going to *say* you're prospering. You must learn to trust *God's* evaluation of your life.

> THERE'S NOTHING THAT SAYS OTHERS ARE GOING TO SAY YOU'RE PROSPERING. YOU MUST TRUST GOD'S EVALUATION OF YOUR LIFE.

You don't need to know the turns your life will take. You don't need the approval of those around you. You don't need to know if your ten-year plan will pan out. You don't even need to know how this prosper-in-all-you-do promise looks in its current fulfillment. The one vital question is this: **Do you trust *Him*?** Do you believe that God cares more about you and your life than you do? Are you constantly thinking on your Lord and His Word and allowing Him to shape and redirect your life? Then this is His promise to you:

You *will* prosper.

TURN THE PAGE
FOR A TIME OF
*Reflection*

**SELF-EXAMINATION:** Friend, if you are among those who doubt the validity of this promise, you're probably not meditating on God's Word day and night. I do not say that as an indictment but as an invitation to step into a life of true prospering. Are you listening to a perishing world's definition of prosperity? Are you doubting the promises of God because of your lack of understanding of what His Word means? Trust His character today. *"He. . .is faithful; He will surely do it"* (1 Thessalonians 5:24). God will fulfill all that He has promised, so don't miss the blessed life by failing to abide in the only place of true abundance—meditating upon His eternal Word.

A TIME FOR

*Reflection*

> *How wonderful Your words, O God, so loving and so true;*
> *They feed our hungry hearts and lives*
> *and fill our thoughts with You.*
> *Beside Your living waters, Lord, we drink a life unseen;*
> *Forever fruitful in Your love, we grow, forever green.*
> *Apart from You, the Source of Life, we blossom for a day;*
> *But rootless, lifeless, all alone, we quickly die away.*
> *You freely share Your wisdom, Lord, and daily prove it true.*
> *We dance today with heaven's joy, for all life is all in You.*[38]

**QUESTIONS TO CONSIDER:** Before addressing these questions, take a few minutes to write down your initial thoughts and reactions to this chapter. What stands out to you? What questions come to mind? What does your flesh initially want to resist?

1. How have you defined *prospering* in the past? Was your definition influenced by the world's perception of prospering?

2. Do you doubt any of the promises of God? Which promises do you struggle to believe? Why might there be doubts?

3. It was said, *"There's nothing here that says you'll feel like you're prospering. There's nothing that says others are going to say you're prospering. You must trust God's evaluation of your life."* How do your feelings sometimes run contrary to what you know to be true?

4. Do you live as one who believes that God's promises are true? Give an example in which your daily life shows that you are relying on God's promises.

5. Do you rely on His Word to show you and remind you of who God is and what His promises are? Are your thoughts about God's character based on what He says about Himself or on what you think He should be like?

6. Take some time to journal on ten promises of God. Start with Psalm 1:3. Now, spend some time considering how your life might be more biblically framed by these truths.

7. How might framing your life around the promises of God bring peace of mind?

## Notes

# THE *Perseverance* OF THE BLESSED MAN

**PSALM 1:1-3**  *Blessed is the man who walks not in the counsel of the wicked, nor stands in the way of sinners, nor sits in the seat of scoffers; but his delight is in the law of the Lord, and on His law he meditates day and night. He is like a tree planted by streams of water that yields its fruit in its season, and **its leaf does not wither**. In all that he does, he prospers.*

**BIG IDEA:**

IF WE ARE PLANTED BY THE STREAMS OF WATER, WE WILL **PERSEVERE** THROUGH EVERY DROUGHT, AND OUR LEAVES WILL NOT WITHER.

How easy it is to grow weary in the work God has called you to do. Have you ever followed the leading of the Lord only to see your plans or ideas seemingly fall apart? I have. In Christ, praise God, we are offered a life that doesn't waver or wither at the constant commotion created by this world, but we are *not* promised a life that constantly produces the results we desire. Today, we encounter the promise of God which guarantees to us that the one who meditates on the law of the Lord will have a leaf which *"does not wither"* (Psalm 1:3).

**WE ARE *NOT* PROMISED A LIFE THAT CONSTANTLY PRODUCES THE RESULTS WE DESIRE.**

Our word is **perseverance**.

*Perseverance* is "persistence in doing something despite difficulty or delay in the journey to achieving success." What will it mean for the tree of our life to have leaves that do not wither? Take one step back: The simple fact that the psalmist includes this detail indicates that the natural tendency of leaves is to wither, to give up, to not persevere, to quit. It is wise for us to be aware of this tendency since we are the trees in this picture and those leaves are on our branches.

Now, back to the green leaves which do *not* wither. What can they teach us about perseverance? Here are four points for our consideration: (1) their condition, (2) their contrast, (3) their comfort, and (4) their consistency.

Leaves serve many purposes, including signaling the **condition** of the tree. This verse speaks of leaves which do not wither, indicating a healthy tree where proper nutrients are being constantly ingested and then distributed throughout the tree's system. This leads us to conclude that withering leaves are the result of a tree *not* receiving its necessary nourishment.

**WITHERING LEAVES ARE THE RESULT OF A TREE *NOT* RECEIVING ITS NECESSARY NOURISHMENT.**

A tree with consistently green leaves *does not* mean that the tree is always bearing fruit, but it *does* indicate that the tree is alive and absorbing the necessary nutrition so that it will bear fruit in the right season. The application is obvious. **We must not give up in the seasons when we aren't seeing the results we want to see!** Hold fast to the truth in Galatians 6:9. *"In due season we will reap, if we do not give up."* Be encouraged! *"The righteous man will flourish like the palm tree, he will grow like a cedar in Lebanon. Planted in the house of the Lord, they will flourish in the courts of our God. They will still yield fruit in old age; they shall be full of sap and very green"* (Psalm 92:12-14 NASB). Not just green, but *"very green."* Did you catch that? This is the *perseverance* of the blessed man; his leaf will not wither. Now consider a couple of **contrasts:**

First, we see the contrast between the leaves and the fruit. This *"tree planted by streams of water"* experiences a continuous inner renewal despite external adversity. While the fruit comes only during certain seasons, the health of this tree is constant; it does not depend on the season. The external results vary, but there is an inner source constantly fueling its

> **THIS TREE "EXPERIENCES A CONTINUOUS INNER RENEWAL DESPITE EXTERNAL ADVERSITY."**

vitality. All this reflects the eternal truth of Jesus' words to the Samaritan woman in John 4:14, *"The water that I will give him will become in him a spring of water welling up to eternal life."* God doesn't just serve us a sample of life; He satisfies us with the Source of Life—Himself.

Wow! In other words, as you meditate on the Lord Himself in all the Scriptures, and as you surrender to the authority of those Scriptures, you, yes you, will be like a tree whose leaves do not wither—no matter how hot and harsh the sun, the situation, or the season. This is because your refreshment and nourishment have nothing to do with your circumstances or the chaos of our culture, *"since you have been born again, not of perishable seed but of imperishable, through the living and abiding word of God; for 'All flesh is like grass and all its glory like the flower of grass. The grass withers, and the flower falls, but the word of the Lord remains forever'"* (1 Peter 1:23-25).

There is another contrast with this particular tree: the blessed versus the wicked. Psalm 1:3 says of the blessed man, *"Its leaf does not wither,"* but verse 4 gives this stark contrast: *"The wicked are not so, but are like chaff that the wind drives away."* The blessed man is lush and verdant, and attached to the Source. The wicked are dry and dead, detached from their life Source—and soon blown away. A clear indicator that a life is not plugged into the Word of God is when that life is shaken by the ever-changing ideas and events of the world. Ephesians 4:14 describes such as one who is *"tossed to and fro by the waves and carried about by every wind of doctrine, by human cunning, by craftiness in deceitful schemes."*

Picture this scene: a place where the ground is dry, the hot winds blow, the rain has ceased, and the leaves are withering and dying on all the trees—*except for one*. There it is. One tree, green and fresh among the dry and dying trees. What a picture of the blessed man in the midst of our dying world! The hot winds of dismissals, disease, discouragement, disappointment, and death are faced by believer and unbeliever alike. Yet there is a difference. One is plugged into the Source of life. The other is not. *"For as **in Adam** all die, so also **in Christ** shall all be made alive"* (1 Corinthians 15:22).

But the picture goes further.

Consider the **comfort** this tree brings. A tree with healthy leaves is more than just *healthy*; it's *helpful*. Even before there is fruit to pick, this tree offers comforting and even vital benefits to its community. Growing up in the Sahel region of West Africa, I experienced the realities of intense heat and the blessing of trees, especially those with an abundance of green, shade-producing, heat-reducing foliage. In most West African villages, you will find a central *meeting place tree*, a large tree under which the villagers gather for the comfort of relief and fellowship. Do people find comfort under our foliage?

**A TREE WITH HEALTHY LEAVES IS MORE THAN JUST *HEALTHY*; IT'S *HELPFUL*.**

Don't believe for a moment that you are of no benefit when your life isn't bringing forth the fruit you expected. As you persevere, plugged into the nourishment of God's Word, just like the rich green leaves of the tree, your very presence can bring relief and refreshment to those who come in contact with you.

**YOUR VERY PRESENCE CAN BRING RELIEF AND REFRESHMENT TO THOSE WHO COME IN CONTACT WITH YOU.**

Finally, think of the **consistency** of such a tree. Whatever the surrounding conditions, it perseveres as it draws daily from the streams of water and goes on growing and bearing fruit, season after season. It abides, and so must you. **We live in a world that praises the famous, but God rewards the faithful. To the one who remains rooted in the Word, God doesn't promise dramatic production, but He does promise perseverance:** *"Its leaf does not wither"* (Psalm 1:3).

Do you allow your season to dictate your faithfulness? **Perseverance is rarely glamorous, but your shade might be just what a weary traveler needs.** To His disciples,

**DO YOU ALLOW YOUR SEASON TO DICTATE YOUR FAITHFULNESS?**

Jesus said, *"As the Father has loved Me, so have I loved you. Abide in My love. If you keep My commandments, you will abide in My love, just as I have kept My Father's commandments and abide in His love. These things I have spoken to you, that My joy may be in you, and that your joy may be full"* (John 15:9-11).

**Your joy is in abiding, not in abundance.** You will persevere as you stay plugged into Him and His Word.

**SELF-EXAMINATION:** Do you speak words of life, even in seasons when you aren't clearly yielding the fruit you perhaps wish you were yielding? Are you a retreat from this world's perspectives, which portray life from temporal and twisted viewpoints, leaving the inner man feeling desperate? Do your friends and acquaintances leave refreshed from a conversation with you? Do others come to you looking for answers, for hope, for refreshment? Peter wrote in his first epistle, *"Always being prepared to make a defense to anyone who asks you for a reason for the hope that is in you"* (1 Peter 3:15). Are people asking about the hope in you? Perhaps they have drawn near to ask because they notice something different about your life. On the other hand, do you at times feel like you are withering? Remember, our responsibility is to be plugged into the Word. God's responsibility is to bring about the fruit in its season.

A TIME FOR

*Reflection*

> *To all life Thou givest, to both great and small;*
> *In all life Thou livest, the true life of all.*
> *We blossom and flourish as leaves on the tree,*
> *And wither and perish, but naught changeth Thee.*[39]

**QUESTIONS TO CONSIDER:** Before addressing these questions, take a few minutes to write down your initial thoughts and reactions to this chapter. What stands out to you? What questions come to mind? What does your flesh initially want to resist?

1. Describe someone who is like a tree that brings refreshment and offers a place to rest. What characteristics of their life stand out?

2. Using your own words, write out a definition for *perseverance*.

3. Where do you go for hope and comfort? Take a few minutes to write out three verses from the Scriptures that you can cling to as a source of nutrition in dry times.

4. Do people come to you during difficult times? What kinds of things do people ask you about (where you buy your clothes, why you vote a certain way, etc.)? Do they ask about your hope? What is your answer?

5. Why is perseverance rarely noted? What is one area in which God has called you to persevere even when your life isn't bearing the fruit you desire?

6. It was mentioned, *"Your joy is in abiding, not in abundance."* How would you explain *abiding* in times when you don't feel like you are abounding?

7. The wicked are described as *"chaff which the wind drives away,"* and the immature are described as being *"tossed to and fro."* How does being plugged into God's Word protect you from being tossed around? Give an example in your life when you were being swayed and persuaded by opinions around you, but the Word of God established your mind.

# Notes

_____
_____
_____
_____
_____
_____
_____
_____
_____
_____
_____
_____
_____
_____
_____
_____
_____
_____
_____
_____

## THE *Power* OF THE BLESSED MAN

**PSALM 1:1-3** *Blessed is the man who walks not in the counsel of the wicked, nor stands in the way of sinners, nor sits in the seat of scoffers; but his delight is in the law of the Lord, and on His law he meditates day and night. He is like a tree planted by streams of water that yields its fruit in its season, and its leaf does not wither. **In all that he does, he prospers.***

**BIG IDEA:**

THE SPIRIT OF GOD IS THE **POWER** WHO ENABLES US TO LIVE A SPIRITUALLY PROSPEROUS LIFE WHICH WILL RESULT IN ETERNAL DIVIDENDS.

From cartoons like Popeye the Sailor, whose source of power is spinach, to Smallville and Superman, who absorbs energy from the yellow sun in order to carry out humanly impossible feats—we're fascinated with the topic of **power**. Imagine having access to a power which guarantees true success—*every time!* Psalm 1 offers us just that, an extraordinary promise that we can enjoy true prosperity, a power that is accessible to any one of us who is willing to make the investment.

**IMAGINE HAVING ACCESS TO A POWER WHICH GUARANTEES TRUE SUCCESS— *EVERY TIME!***

And yet, it's largely ignored.
Even by those who claim to believe it.

We are focusing now on the last phrase of Psalm 1:3, *"In all that he does, he prospers."* The terminology employed and the totality, the extensiveness, of the statement both deserve a closer look.

First, the **terminology**. The meaning of the Hebrew word used here for *prospers* opens before us various spheres of this precious promise of God for the blessed man. Furthermore, it gives us an understanding of God's will for those who meditate on the Word. Consider athletes who desire to excel in their sport. They don't become great by simply desiring to become great. Rather, greatness will be a by-product of their investment of time, energy, and passion in training, practicing, and playing their sport. Likewise, the promised power of prospering is the direct result of soaking in and responding to God's Word.

> THE PROMISED POWER OF PROSPERING IS THE DIRECT RESULT OF SOAKING IN AND RESPONDING TO GOD'S WORD.

The word is *tsalach*, and it has several nuances. From a military perspective, it means "to attack" or "fall upon." To a traveler, it might mean "going over or through a river." A third dimension of this word is actually missional, and it carries the idea of "finishing well."

Regardless of the definition you latched onto, the meaning is clear. **Prospering is not something that passively happens to you. It is the result of an action which you choose to take.** Furthermore, there must be a power source behind the action to fuel and sustain it. Psalm 1 does not depict an idle man waiting for God to bless him, nor an individual who feels privileged, entitled, or even deprived. Rather, it portrays a man in pursuit, the pursuit

> PROSPERING IS THE RESULT OF AN ACTION WHICH YOU CHOOSE TO TAKE.

of knowing his God. He is aiming to finish well by meditating day and night on the precepts of his God.

God promises that true prosperity will result from continual meditation on His Word—including prioritization, preoccupation, and practice. What an encouragement to recognize that this power is not of ourselves! The gospel is not a message of "Try harder!" Rather, the power of God to salvation is accessed in, and only in, the finished work of Jesus Christ (see Romans 1:16). And the power for those who are in Christ to live a spiritually prosperous life comes from the Spirit of God. He is the Source and the Fuel who produces fruit in us that will inevitably change lives around us.

The question is, "Do we believe that change in this chaotic world can come through humble surrender to the eternal Word of God?" We are reminded in Hebrews 4:12, *"For the word of God is living and active, sharper than any two-edged sword, piercing to the division of soul and of spirit, of joints and of marrow, and discerning the thoughts and intentions of the heart."* Meditating on God's law may not seem like a remarkable act, but the One who *"cannot deny Himself"* (2 Timothy 2:13) promises that the one who does exactly that *will* prosper.

**MEDITATING ON GOD'S LAW MAY NOT SEEM LIKE A REMARKABLE ACT, BUT THE ONE WHO DOES EXACTLY THAT *WILL* PROSPER.**

But the promise goes even further. Dwell on the **totality** of this promise, the extent to which it reaches: *"In all that he does, he prospers"* (Psalm 1:3). If you don't trust the Lord, you'll say, "That's impossible! It's an unbelievable promise!" But you must adopt His definition of prospering. If you don't, you'll try it and say, "It's false!" Try it. **Trust the Master Gardener, take up the call, and you will bear fruit in season and prosper in all that you do.**

Now grab onto this word.
*All.*

Those who choose to trust His Word won't get bogged down by constant questions of "What might have been?" They can be assured that the eternal dividends of such a pursuit are well worth the investment. They can be assured that the result of the blessed life will be powerful, not according to man's opinion, but according to the supreme measure of God's eternal Word.

**SELF-EXAMINATION:** Have you aligned your thinking with God's definition of prospering? It can be tempting to ask, "How is having cancer *prospering*?" Maybe you look at your income and question, "How is this *prospering*?" Perhaps you are aching in spirit right now. You're emotionally fractured and wondering, "How can this be defined, in any way, as *prospering*?" My mind goes to my brothers and sisters around the world who, today, will die for the name of the Lord Jesus Christ. We could ask, "How is *that* prospering?" The answer? **Prospering has *nothing*, I repeat, *nothing* to do with earthly ease or enjoyment. Prospering does not require approval, affirmation, or affection from others. Prospering does not promise the abundance of things or travel. Prospering doesn't promise safety, earthly stability, or status.** Instead, Psalm 1:3 makes it clear that prospering is bearing fruit. Prospering is knowing your God. Prospering is found in constantly receiving the life-giving nutrients from God's Spirit through His Word. And prospering is knowing that, when this life is through, *"I shall dwell in the house of the Lord forever"* (Psalm 23:6). Rest in God's promises. Saturate yourself with His Word, not with worldly success, and God will make you to prosper in the true sense of the word.

A TIME FOR

*Reflection*

*Praise to the Lord, who doth prosper thy work and defend thee,*
*Who, from the heavens, the streams of His mercy doth send thee.*
*Ponder anew what the Almighty can do, who with His love doth befriend thee.*[40]

**QUESTIONS TO CONSIDER:** Before addressing these questions, take a few minutes to write down your initial thoughts and reactions to this chapter. What stands out to you? What questions come to mind? What does your flesh initially want to resist?

1. Think of superheroes and their powers. Now, consider the power God has given us through His Word. Do you commonly think less of God's power than you do of the power of fictional characters on the big screen? Explain.

2. Do your best to accurately describe *prospering* from a non-biblical worldview. Now, take the definition shared in this chapter and juxtapose (compare) the two. What striking contrasts do you see?

3. How would you define *power*? Who or what is influencing your perception of true power?

4. You learned three aspects of the biblical term *to prosper*—from a military mindset, a traveler's perspective, and a missional viewpoint. Which one resonates most with you, and why?

5. How do your circumstances and feelings cause your perception of *prospering* to fluctuate?

6. Where in your life do you feel like you are prospering according to Psalm 1:3? How does this look and what defines it as *prospering*?

7. What keeps followers of Christ from prospering? Be specific, beyond the answer, "They aren't meditating on God's Word day and night." Make it personal. What keeps you from prospering?

# Notes

# THE *Perspective* OF THE BLESSED MAN

**PSALM 1:1-3**    *Blessed is the man who walks not in the counsel of the wicked, nor stands in the way of sinners, nor sits in the seat of scoffers; but his delight is in the law of the Lord, and on His law he meditates day and night. **He is like a tree** planted by streams of water that yields its fruit in its season, and its leaf does not wither. In all that he does, he prospers.*

**BIG IDEA:**

OUR EARTHLY LIVES GAIN AN ETERNAL **PERSPECTIVE** WHEN WE LOOK AT EVERYTHING FROM GOD'S HEAVENLY POINT OF VIEW.

Look at something. Anything. What do you see? Ask a young child this question, and you'll get one answer—probably a straightforward one. Ask an engineer, and you'll get another answer—perhaps a technical one. Ask a minister, and I expect you'll get yet a different answer—and it'll probably be a fair bit longer.

Now, turn your focus from whatever it was, and look at the tree of Psalm 1 through the lens of imagination. But don't just focus on the tree. I ask you to fly the drone of your mind to a point higher than the tree so that you are now looking down on it from above. **Perspective** is an interesting phenomenon. And this is the topic we aim to enjoy as we turn our eyes once more to Psalm 1 and the blessed life.

The etymology of the word *perspective* is really based on the two words "through" and "to look." Perspective is not just a matter of seeing; **it involves seeing beyond the obvious**. I think of three words in association with this idea of perspective: (1) invisible, (2) impactful, and (3) imperishable. These are the fruit of true perspective. I'll explain.

First, **invisible.**

When you sweep your gaze over the landscape of any terrain, what generally stands high above other things? More often than not, it is trees. When I was a child, trees were one of my favorite hang-outs. We had seven Sapote ["Sap-o-tee"] trees (bearing an exotic West African fruit) in our backyard. Many a day, I would climb high into their branches, often with a book, find a nook, and settle in for a good read. If my mom came looking for me, she would  have to call out into the yard because there was no seeing me. I loved the spot not only for its privacy but also for its view. Through the leaves, my perch gave me a much wider perspective of my surroundings. I saw things that I otherwise would have missed. Though I was hidden in the leaves, from my new perspective, things once invisible to me could now be seen and enjoyed.

Concerning perspective, the apostle Paul reminds us, *"We look not to the things that are seen but to the things that are unseen. For the things that are seen are transient, but the things that are unseen are eternal"* (2 Corinthians 4:18). So how is the blessed man enabled to see the unseen? He looks through the eyes of faith, drawing from the pure streams of the Word of God, then acting on that Word. It is God's Word which gives us His eternal perspective, a perspective invisible to earthly eyes, a perspective from above.

**IT IS GOD'S WORD WHICH GIVES US HIS ETERNAL PERSPECTIVE.**

And so Psalm 1 tells us that the blessed man *"is like a tree"* (Psalm 1:3): like a tree that stands above the landscape, like a tree that offers a *perspective* of things not otherwise seen. And when we walk in obedience to God's Word through the power of the Holy Spirit, we will prosper as we soak in the view from that God-given perspective, the view of things that are otherwise invisible.

> Secondly, the blessed man's perspective is **impactful**.

The reality is that our world is a confused, chaotic place. Consider society's thoughts and ways. Are they illogical? At times. Irresponsible? Oftentimes. Irreverent? Most of the time. Thus, we must be cautious. If I respond to the world with the perspective of the world, that is, in my flesh, I will react in frustration, sarcasm, anger, or even animosity. But Jesus said, *"I say to you who hear, Love your enemies, do good to those who hate you, bless those who curse you, pray for those who abuse you"* (Luke 6:27-28).

How is such a response even possible? I must choose to view others through the lens of the heart and the Word of the Lord. These instruct my mind and heart, teaching me that all people everywhere have been knit together by their Creator and are loved by Him with an everlasting love— to the degree that God sent His own Son to suffer and die, *for them*, taking upon Himself the whole of their sin. **If I want to see the world around me as God sees it, I must be like the tree planted by streams of water, the tree that rises above its surrounding terrain in order to gain a proper perspective—**

**I MUST CHOOSE TO VIEW OTHERS THROUGH THE LENS OF THE HEART AND THE WORD OF THE LORD.**

**God's perspective, the eternal picture.** This perspective can strongly impact our perception of life!

Finally, the **imperishable**.

I want to live a life that counts forever. I want to live in such a way that my life's dividends multiply exponentially upon my death. Jesus spoke of that opportunity when He said, *"Do not lay up for yourselves treasures on earth, where moth and rust destroy and where thieves break in and steal, but lay up for yourselves treasures in heaven where neither moth nor rust destroys and where thieves do not break in and steal"* (Matthew 6:19-20). We are invited to look upon life from the perspective of eternity, to understand the eternal repercussions of the responses we make here on earth.

**I WANT TO LIVE IN SUCH A WAY THAT MY LIFE'S DIVIDENDS MULTIPLY EXPONENTIALLY UPON MY DEATH.**

We considered in a previous chapter the blessing that healthy leaves are to others. But what blocks your view when climbing a tree? Leaves. Leaves are good, but they admittedly often got in the way of my seeing clearly from my perch in those Sapote trees. Similarly, **more often than not, even the good things in life can block our perspective of the eternal—leaves such as misplaced priorities, misappropriated affections, or misaligned goals.** But the leaves don't necessarily have to be removed; they're just in the way.

What is the solution?
Climb higher!
And how can you do that?

Let God's Word instruct you and change your perspective. **His truth will allow you to rise above the distortion caused by the many leaves, above the world's confusion, and above your own circumstances as well.**

Are we like the blessed man who meditates on that worldview-transforming Word day and night? If so, we will gain the perspective of the imperishable—of the things that really count. In what areas do we view life from a wrong perspective? How can you tell if your perspective is out of sync with God's perspective? Here's a clue. In what circumstances do you ever feel hatred toward another? In what situations do you yield to despair? François Fénelon said it well: "Accustom yourself to unreasonableness and injustice. Abide in peace in the presence of God Who sees all these evils more clearly than you do, and Who permits them. Be content with doing with calmness the little which depends upon yourself, and let all else be to you as if it were naught." [41]

> "ABIDE IN PEACE IN THE PRESENCE OF GOD WHO SEES ALL THESE EVILS MORE CLEARLY THAN YOU DO, AND WHO PERMITS THEM."

**My friend, when your perspective does not allow you to see in a circumstance its potential to turn out for God's glory and your eternal good, it's time to climb higher by digging deeper into the treasure of God's Word.**

TURN THE PAGE FOR A TIME OF
*Reflection*

**SELF-EXAMINATION:** Take a few moments to check your surroundings to see if your perspective is clear. Are you seeing through the leaves? Are you seeing through your circumstances? Are you seeing through a news report, a doctor's diagnosis, or the current opinion of someone else? Are you even climbing the tree? The Word will have the last word, because that Word endures forever. Seeing this life and this world from God's perspective, through what He has said, will result in clear vision and a renewed focus and hope.

A TIME FOR

*Reflection*

> *Time is filled with swift transition,*
> *Naught of earth unmoved can stand.*
> *Build your hopes on things eternal.*
> *Hold to God's unchanging hand.*[42]

**QUESTIONS TO CONSIDER: Before addressing these questions, take a few minutes to write down your initial thoughts and reactions to this chapter. What stands out to you? What questions come to mind? What does your flesh initially want to resist?**

1. What do you see? Consider a current news story. What does it look like from ground level? Now, climb the tree of meditating on God's law. How does this new perspective change your possible response and actions?

2. What leaves, though good and useful, block your view so that you cannot see your situation clearly?

3. What practical disciplines (for example, putting a verse on your mirror, being slow to speak, or recognizing God's constant presence in every moment) might help you to see the invisible in your daily life?

4. How might you climb higher to see from God's perspective by digging deeper into His Word?

5. Is your perspective on [insert circumstance or issue] you-centered or God-focused?

6. Where do you allow your human understanding of a particular thing to stop you from seeing from God's perspective and changing your own? Are you in a rut that keeps you from accepting God's bigger and perfect viewpoint? What areas of your life do you identify as being unworthy of God due to a limited perspective (perhaps in holiness, relationships, career, or time consumption)?

7. Give an example or two from Scripture of a character who saw beyond their situation and didn't let their circumstances control their mindset.

# Notes

# THE *Portal* OF THE BLESSED MAN

**PSALM 1:1-3** *Blessed is the man who walks not in the counsel of the wicked, nor stands in the way of sinners, nor sits in the seat of scoffers; but his delight is in the law of the Lord, and on His law he meditates day and night. He is like a tree planted by streams of water that yields its fruit in its season, and its leaf does not wither. **In all that he does, he prospers.***

**BIG IDEA:**

THE ONE WHO DESIRES DEEP INTIMACY WITH GOD WILL ENTER THROUGH THE **PORTAL** OF PRAYER INTO A MOMENT-BY-MOMENT LIVING IN HIS VERY PRESENCE.

common children's activity is that of drawing a picture by connecting the dots. Each dot is numbered and the child has to simply draw a line from one number to the next. The result at the end will be the revelation of an image. If the dots are not connected in sequence, the picture will be messed up and the image will be lost. In a similar manner, we can easily fail to "connect the dots" in the Word of God.

How common it is to separate spiritual disciplines, to isolate passages, to simply miss how one idea links to another. Consider, for example, our previous discussion on true blessedness. What cause and effect link have we found in Scripture concerning this subject? We've learned that blessedness is a by-product of meditating on God's Word day and night. Yet how many of us are trying to obtain this blessedness by simply aiming for it? By properly connecting the dots, we see that this can never work. Now we're about to discover another vital aspect of our life in Christ which is also a by-product of that same decision to meditate on God's Word.

Consider the **portal** of the blessed man.

A *portal* is "a doorway, a gate, or an entrance." This definition is key, so listen up. Let's start with a question. How would you describe your prayer life? Most Christians see their prayer life as one of their weakest disciplines in their daily walk with the Lord. And, interestingly, it is generally those who have a strong prayer life who crave a deeper intimacy with God since they have tasted of its sweetness and long for more. Let's take a step forward toward the door to prayer and take some time to consider this portal to a fruitful, healthy, and prospering life.

The portal into prayer.

How and where is prayer addressed in Psalm 1:2-3? Another question might be helpful. In whose presence do we find ourself in Psalm 1:2-3? As we meditate day and night on the Word, we are *"like a tree planted by streams of water."* We are camped out in the presence of God. Therefore, the very invitation to meditate on God's Word is an invitation to dwell in God's presence. The implications are startling.

**THE VERY INVITATION TO MEDITATE ON GOD'S WORD IS AN INVITATION TO DWELL IN GOD'S PRESENCE.**

I have numerous friends who have made the marvelous choice to adopt a child. In some cases, the adoptions have been international. One particular couple, American citizens, adopted a precious newborn daughter from Korea. Let me tell you what these folks *didn't* declare upon adoption. They didn't say, "Now we are going to take Korean classes so that when our daughter starts to talk we will understand her language." Obviously not! Though their child was from Korea, she did not start speaking Korean. Her mother tongue was English, the language of her adopting family. She learned and speaks the language in which she was raised.

So it is for us as we meditate on the Word. We are like that baby who heard the voices, the words, and the expressed thoughts of her parents and who learned to respond in the same language. As a tree planted by streams of water, we hear God's thoughts on life and come to know His heart for us, and we learn to speak back. Prayer is, ultimately, a response to God's Word. In the words of John, the apostle and disciple of Christ, *"We love because He first loved us"* (I John 4:19).

> **AS A TREE PLANTED BY STREAMS OF WATER, WE HEAR GOD'S THOUGHTS ON LIFE AND COME TO KNOW HIS HEART FOR US, AND WE LEARN TO SPEAK BACK.**

It is critical to understand that this is more than just an interesting perspective on the Word of God. It is a *practical necessity.* If we fail to be in the Word, our prayer life will be molded by our earthly culture and traditions or, even more tragically, by our volatile feelings. **The purest portal into prayer is God's Word as it alone enables us to understand and know our God and to respond to His heart rather than react to our circumstances.**

As we learn to pray for God's will to be done on earth as it is in heaven, we eventually come to understand that this is not about our preferences; it is about His glory, and it's all *for* His glory. **Tragically, many believers see prayer primarily as an emergency calling system rather than as an invitation to moment-by-moment intimacy with God.** Life is not meant to merely *include* devotions. Rather, we are to live **a devotional life.** We might also say that we do not need a *prayer life*; instead, we have been summoned to **a life of prayer**. To truly prosper, to have intimacy with the Almighty, is the result of *a life*, not merely a moment here and there, being planted by the streams of water, meditating on the pure Word of God.

**WE DO NOT NEED A *PRAYER LIFE*; INSTEAD, WE HAVE BEEN SUMMONED TO *A LIFE OF PRAYER*.**

Going back to our introductory question, "How would you describe your prayer life?" allow me to add a second question. "How would you *define* prayer?" When Jesus spoke of prayer, He most often used the word *proseuchomai*. This compound word has been described as "interacting with the Lord by turning toward Him, and exchanging human wishes or ideas for His wishes as He imparts faith."

Picture this. **If we turn our face toward God, we will simultaneously be turning our face away from other things**. Every day we are bombarded by people's opinions, our own doubts, the discouragements of current events, and the chaos of a very loud world. Prayer is the salve for our disease of restlessness. God invites us into His presence so He might change our perspective, calm our hearts, and conform our life to His. **Prayer isn't primarily concerned with the syntax of our words before God. What we say in His presence is not primarily what brings about change in us. Rather, it's about what we see in His presence and our response to it.** When we see God clearly, we see our circumstances differently. It is easy to

**GOD INVITES US INTO HIS PRESENCE SO HE MIGHT CHANGE OUR PERSPECTIVE, CALM OUR HEARTS, AND CONFORM OUR LIFE TO HIS.**

claim the second half of Psalm 37:4, *"He will give you the desires of your heart,"* but are we ignoring the prerequisite? ***"Delight yourself in the Lord...."***

We may wonder how it is possible to obey the words of Christ in Luke 18:1 where Jesus tells us that people *"ought always to pray,"* or again, in I Thessalonians 5:17, where Paul tells the church that they are to *"pray without ceasing."* But these commands align perfectly with the man of Psalm 1 who meditates on the law of the Lord day and night. Always. Without ceasing. Day and night.

**WE "OUGHT ALWAYS TO PRAY." *ALWAYS.* WITHOUT CEASING. DAY AND NIGHT. CONSISTENCY AND CONSTANCY.**

Consistency and constancy.

My wife and I begin our day with a "Good morning!" but, as the day progresses, we don't continue to greet each other every time we interact. If we see a beautiful sight as we travel, we may discuss it, but we don't begin with, "Hi, Dear! How are you? Isn't that architecture stunning?" As our stomachs begin to growl and food begins to sound like a good idea, I don't say, "Good afternoon, Wife! How are you? Would you like a bite to eat?" If we are lost, I may ask my wife to pull up some directions on her phone, but I certainly don't, in my haste, begin with, "Hi, Sweetheart! I hope you're doing fine today. Say, I think we are lost!"

Why do we dispense with such formalities? It's because we've already passed through the portal to communication. My mind and my heart have already been aligned with hers. We are "in communion" and communication. Now apply this to God. This is how it is meant to be with your prayer life—with your *life of prayer.* That is the blessed man of Psalm 1. He has gone through the door and has entered into communion with God. He is now passing everything through the filter of God's Word, God's mind, God's heart.

He has entered the portal.

**Many believers ask God for intimacy but refuse to enter the portal. We want to know God, but we refuse to camp out in the place where He communicates.** We desire intimacy, but we think it an inconvenience to meditate on His Word.

This psalm is a Fatherly invitation to go through the doorway, the portal, so that we might enter into the fullness of life as His daughter or as His son. We are invited inside the palace of the King of the universe, not only positionally in Christ, but also practically through His Word. In fact, He invites us right into His throne-room to listen in on His divine conversations by entering through the portal of meditation on His Word and surrendering to the conviction of His Holy Spirit. There, He will share His thoughts with us as we walk with Him and enjoy living in His presence, not just for a few minutes or even an hour or two in the morning, but continuously, day and night. **When we see God's glory clearly—His grace, His power, His unfailing love, His plan, and His eternity—it will change our understanding of the events and burdens of life around us. Walking through the portal of prayer will be our natural longing and response.**

WE ARE INVITED INSIDE THE PALACE OF THE KING OF THE UNIVERSE. HE INVITES US RIGHT INTO HIS THRONE-ROOM TO LISTEN IN ON HIS DIVINE CONVERSATIONS.

This is the life of the blessed man.

**SELF-EXAMINATION:** Do you desire to know God's heart so that you might speak with Him about His desires? When you are in the Word, do you pray back to God what He has already said to you? How are you actively learning to communicate with Him through the portal of prayer? How might your definition of prayer be more about you than about Him? How do you use meditation on God's Word as a portal to your life of prayer? Have you ever had the idea that to "pray without ceasing" is an impossible task (as though it hinged on your performance rather than on your placement by the stream of His Word)?

*I come to the garden alone*
*While the dew is still on the roses,*
*And the voice I hear falling on my ear,*
*The Son of God discloses.*
*He speaks and the sound of His voice*
*Is so sweet the birds hush their singing,*
*And the melody that He gave to me,*
*Within my heart is ringing.*
*And He walks with me, and He talks with me,*
*And He tells me I am His own;*
*And the joy we share as we tarry there,*
*None other has ever known.*[43]

**QUESTIONS TO CONSIDER: Before addressing these questions, take a few minutes to write down your initial thoughts and reactions to this chapter. What stands out to you? What questions come to mind? What does your flesh initially want to resist?**

1. In this chapter, what challenged your view on prayer?

2. How would you currently describe your prayer life? Write it out.

3. How might you be avoiding the portal of prayer? Give specific examples.

4. What might it look like throughout the day to *"pray without ceasing"* (1 Thessalonians 5:17)? Try journaling through a day to see what distracts you from seeing everything in His presence and through His Word?

5. What (relationship, conversation, plan, etc.) might drastically change in your daily routine if you were to choose to enter through the portal Psalm 1 lays before you?

6. Prayer was described in this chapter as *"interacting with the Lord by turning toward Him, and exchanging human wishes or ideas for His wishes as He imparts faith."* What exchange of ideas or wishes might God want from you today?

7. If you claim Christ to be preeminent in your life, does your day-to-day prayer life (or life of prayer!) reflect this claim?

# Notes

_____
_____
_____
_____
_____
_____
_____
_____
_____
_____
_____
_____
_____
_____
_____
_____
_____
_____
_____
_____
_____
_____

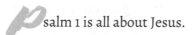

# THE *Portrait* OF THE BLESSED MAN

**PSALM 1:1-3** *Blessed is the man who walks not in the counsel of the wicked, nor stands in the way of sinners, nor sits in the seat of scoffers; but his delight is in the law of the Lord, and on His law he meditates day and night. He is like a tree planted by streams of water that yields its fruit in its season, and its leaf does not wither. In all that he does, he prospers.*

**BIG IDEA:**

THE LORD JESUS CHRIST IS THE PERFECT **PORTRAIT** OF THE TRULY BLESSED MAN— THE ONE WHO MEDITATED DAY AND NIGHT IN THE LAW OF THE LORD, WHOSE LEAVES NEVER WITHERED, AND WHO PROSPERS ETERNALLY IN THE PERFECT WILL OF THE FATHER.

*P*salm 1 is all about Jesus.

Jesus Christ said, *"You search the Scriptures because you think that in them you have eternal life; and it is they that bear witness about Me"* (John 5:39). With this summary statement from the Gospel of John, we introduce our final contemplation of the blessed man of Psalm 1. Yes, we have caught many glimpses of this blessed person, but we have yet to scale the pinnacle.

How does Psalm 1 point us to, and reveal to us, our wonderful Savior and Lord?

In his book *The Man Christ Jesus*,[44] Dr. Bruce Ware calls Christ the *"Psalm 1 prototype."* Why? Psalm 1 describes the blessed man, but, if it were not for the Lord Jesus Christ, no such blessing could ever be possible. Jesus Himself is *The* Blessed Man. What a contrast exists between *"the man"* of Psalm 1 (masculine, singular) versus *"the wicked"* (plural). There, alone, stands One who is altogether separate from the sinful state and practices of the world around him. But for the grace of God, *"the wicked"* would include all of us, forever, for the Word of God tells us, *"None is righteous, no, not one; no one understands; no one seeks for God. All have turned aside; together they have become worthless"* (Romans 3:10-12). The question posed by the early prophet Job rings out in response: *"How then can man be in the right before God?"* (Job 25:4).

As we have been reminded in our considerations of the blessed man, our righteous position before God has not come by our fulfillment of all the principles set before us in Psalm 1; it has come only through faith in Christ. The true Blessed Man never sinned, yet God made Him to be the offering for our sin, *"so that in Him we might become the righteousness of God"* (2 Corinthians 5:21). Thus, we can say, *"Therefore, since we have been justified by faith, we have peace with God through our Lord Jesus Christ.... For while we were still weak, at the right time Christ died for the ungodly"* (Romans 5:1,6). In the moment that we believed this good news, God blessed us *"in Christ with every spiritual blessing"* (Ephesians 1:3) and invited us to enjoy those heavenly blessings in relationship with Him for time and eternity.

How is all this possible? *"The Word became flesh and dwelt among us"* (John 1:14). Christ Himself is the Word, the Law of the Lord, the very heart of God—in Person, in the flesh. As part of Adam's fallen family, we are by nature among the *"wicked* [who] *will not stand in* [endure/survive] *the judgment"* (Psalm 1:5). But in Christ, The Blessed Man, we are declared righteous. He alone *never* walked in the counsel of the wicked; He *never* stood in the way of

> **CHRIST, *THE* BLESSED MAN ALONE *NEVER* WALKED IN THE COUNSEL OF THE WICKED NOR STOOD IN THE WAY OF SINNERS; HE *NEVER* SAT IN THE SEAT OF SCOFFERS.**

sinners; He *never* sat in the seat of scoffers (Psalm 1:1). But through the forgiveness and righteousness He credits to us when we trust in His finished work, we are invited into the intimacy of knowing and enjoying Him—today and forever. We are invited to be in union with Him—for time and for eternity!

Jesus Christ is the One who flawlessly meditated on the Word day and night.

At age 12, He was in the temple discussing the law of the Lord. He spent His early mornings in solitude and silence, communing with His Father. This was His food, as He says in John 4:34, *"My food is to do the will of Him who sent Me and to accomplish His work."* When tempted in the desert, Jesus responded, *"Man shall not live by bread alone, but by every word that comes from the mouth of God"* (Matthew 4:4). The Lord Jesus, God incarnate, used the Word to defeat the devil, to walk with His Father, and to enjoy intimacy with Him. *We have these same resources*. Pause. Be amazed. We have His Word. We have His Spirit. We have His example, *so that* we *"might follow in His steps"* (1 Peter 2:21).

**WE HAVE THE SAME RESOURCES. PAUSE. BE AMAZED. WE HAVE HIS WORD. WE HAVE HIS SPIRIT. WE HAVE HIS EXAMPLE,**

Jesus Christ is the Portrait, the Prototype, and the Person of Psalm 1.

Though He was God in flesh, He obeyed as man. In Psalm 40:8 He said prophetically, *"I delight to do Your will, O my God; Your law is within My heart."* This was evidenced by Jesus' frequent quoting of the Old Testament Scriptures. The Lord Jesus meditated on the law of the Lord day and night.

Are we assuming that we can navigate life any differently than the ultimate Blessed Man of Psalm 1? Again, I ask, do we consider meditating on God's Word to be a good idea or an absolute necessity? If ever there was One who was *"planted by streams of water that yields its fruit in its season,"* it is the Lord Jesus Christ. But think of *His* version of prospering. Isaiah 53:10 tells us, *"Yet it was the will of the Lord to crush Him; He has put Him to grief; when His soul makes an offering for guilt, He shall see His offspring, He shall prolong His days; the will of the Lord shall* **prosper** *in His hand."* **For Christ, prospering meant doing the will of God, even unto death, so that we might prosper by knowing and enjoying Him forever.**

Let's not quickly forget that aspect of prospering which has to do with "finishing well." Upon the cross, Jesus declared, *"It is finished!"* (John 19:30). And in chorus with the crowds of Mark 7:37, we declare, *"He has done all things well!"*

I don't want to stretch the picture, but I cannot help but think again of *the tree. "He shall be like a tree"* (Psalm 1:3). Think of it. This tree we have been considering in Psalm 1 offers hope and life to the world. A tree absorbs carbon dioxide and expels oxygen. A tree takes in the harmful and releases the good necessary for life. This is what Jesus did for us. He is The Blessed Man, the Tree that offers the fruit by which others taste God's goodness, mercy, and forgiveness which bring us into eternal life. Concerning all who believe, God says, *"He will see the fruit of His suffering and will be satisfied"* (Isaiah 53:11 Masoretic Text). As Jesus affirmed to Nicodemous, *"As Moses*

> A TREE ABSORBS CARBON DIOXIDE AND EXPELS OXYGEN. A TREE TAKES IN THE HARMFUL AND RELEASES THE GOOD NECESSARY FOR LIFE. THIS IS WHAT JESUS DID FOR US.

*lifted up the serpent in the wilderness, so must the Son of Man be lifted up, that whoever believes in Him may have eternal life"* (John 3:14-15). It was for our sins that Christ, The Blessed Man, was lifted up on the cross, called a *tree* in 1 Peter 2:24. But the story didn't end there. *"For as by a man came death, by a man has come also the resurrection of the dead. For as in Adam all die, so also in Christ shall all be made alive. But each in his own order: Christ the firstfruits, then at His coming those who belong to Christ"* (1 Corinthians 15:21-23).

**IT WAS FOR OUR SINS THAT CHRIST, THE BLESSED MAN, WAS LIFTED UP ON THE CROSS, CALLED A TREE. BUT THE STORY DIDN'T END THERE!**

And so the risen Lord says to us today, *"Truly, truly, I say to you, whoever hears My word and believes Him who sent Me has eternal life. He does not come into judgment, but has passed from death to life"* (John 5:24). And, *"Fear not, I am the first and the last, and the living one. I died, and behold I am alive forevermore, and I have the keys of Death and Hades"* (Revelation 1:17-18).

For all eternity, we will sing of, and to, this Blessed Man who *"is like [that] tree planted by streams of water that yields its fruit in its season, and its leaf does not wither.* **In all that he does, he prospers***"* (Psalm 1:3). He will share His prosperity with His redeemed people, His bride—united in intimate fellowship forever. *"For you know the grace of our Lord Jesus Christ, that though He was rich, yet for your sake He became poor, so that you by His poverty might become rich"* (2 Corinthians 8:9).

**FOR ALL ETERNITY, WE WILL SING *OF*, AND *TO*, THIS BLESSED MAN WHO "IS LIKE [THAT] TREE. IN ALL THAT HE DOES, HE PROSPERS."**

To get a glimpse of His prosperity, let's move to the final chapter of the law of the Lord, the Bible:

> *Then the angel showed me the river of the water of life, bright as crystal, flowing from the throne of God and of the Lamb through the middle of the street of the city; also, on either side of the river, **the tree of life** with its twelve kinds of fruit, yielding its fruit each month. The leaves of the tree were for the healing of the nations. No longer will there be anything accursed, but the throne of God and of the Lamb will be in it, and His servants will worship Him. They will see His face, and His name will be on their foreheads. And night will be no more. They will need no light of lamp or sun, for the Lord God will be their light, and they will reign forever and ever* (Revelation 22:1-5).

What a future is ours! Meditate on it. Intimacy with our Creator-Redeemer—*forever!*

This same final chapter of God's Book concludes with an invitation into that intimacy from the Blessed Man Himself. *"Blessed are those who wash their robes, so that they may have the right to the tree of life and that they may enter the city by the gates. The Spirit and the Bride say, 'Come.' And let the one who hears say, 'Come.' And let the one who is thirsty come; let the one who desires take the water of life without price. He who testifies to these things says, 'Surely I am coming soon.' Amen. Come, Lord Jesus!"* (Revelation 22:14,17,20).

Clearly, this is no self-help psalm which says, "Try harder." If it were, we would quickly become exhausted. Nor is it a call to simply "Imitate Jesus!" If it were, we would grow discouraged as we so thoroughly fail to meet His perfect standard. This is an invitation into the righteousness of God, through faith in the blood of Jesus Christ, shed for you and me. This is an invitation from God to enjoy a relationship with Him forever.

**CLEARLY, THIS IS NO SELF-HELP PSALM WHICH SAYS, "TRY HARDER." NOR IS IT A CALL TO SIMPLY "IMITATE JESUS!"**

We had no hope of the blessed life apart from the truth of Psalm 32:2, *"Blessed is the man against whom the Lord counts no iniquity."* There is no blessed life outside of Jesus Christ, *The Blessed Man.* He invites you into His life—into an intimacy to be enjoyed, relished, today and throughout eternity. *"As it is written, 'What no eye has seen, nor ear heard, nor the heart of man imagined, what God has prepared for those who love Him'—these things God has revealed to us through the Spirit. For the Spirit searches everything, even the depths of God"* (1 Corinthians 2:9-10).

TURN THE PAGE
FOR A TIME OF
*Reflection*

**SELF-EXAMINATION:** Have you lost sight of The True Blessed Man in your quest for a blessed life? Where are you trying to earn something from God through your performance rather than trusting His Word, His love, and His grace that flow freely from Christ's finished work? Are you resting in Christ, or are you restless in this world? As we meditate on the Word day and night, we too will reflect our Savior, bearing fruit, withering not, and prospering in all we do. To sum it up: That Blessed Man, the Lord Jesus Christ, has perfectly and forever blessed all who trust in Him. So, until we are forever with Him, let us live the blessed life, planted in the law of the Lord, bearing fruit in season, and prospering in all that we do.

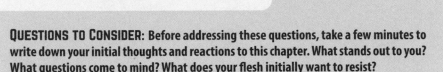

A TIME FOR

*Reflection*

*Fairest of all the earth beside, chiefest of all unto Thy bride,*
*Fullness divine in Thee I see, beautiful Man of Calvary!*

*Granting the sinner life and peace, granting the captive sweet release,*
*Shedding His blood to make us free, merciful Man of Calvary!*

*Comfort of all my earthly way, Jesus, I'll meet Thee some sweet day;*
*Center of glory, Thee I'll see, wonderful Man of Calvary!*

*That Man of Calvary, has won my heart from me,*
*And died to set me free, **Blessed Man** of Calvary!* [45]

**QUESTIONS TO CONSIDER: Before addressing these questions, take a few minutes to write down your initial thoughts and reactions to this chapter. What stands out to you? What questions come to mind? What does your flesh initially want to resist?**

1. Have you placed your faith in The Blessed Man of Psalm 1? Write out your story, your testimony, of trusting Jesus as your Savior and as your Source of true blessedness.

2. How are you encouraged by knowing that this psalm is not one of self-help or of trying harder, but one that points us to true rest?

3. Do you take Christ's sacrifice for granted? How have you lost the wonder of God's love for you as demonstrated through Jesus Christ? Think through your day. How does His work on your behalf impact the way you spend your moments?

4. Is there an area of your life where are you trying to earn something from God through your performance rather than trusting His Word, His love, and His grace? Explain.

5. In what ways might you be pursuing a blessed life instead of pursuing The Blessed Man Himself?

6. What thoughts from Psalm 1 have impacted your life?

7. List three practical applications you want to apply to your life as a result of this study.

# Notes

_____
_____
_____
_____
_____
_____
_____
_____
_____
_____
_____
_____
_____
_____
_____
_____
_____
_____

## *Appendix I*

# DIVING INTO SCRIPTURE

*This Book of the Law shall not depart from your mouth,*
*but you shall meditate on it day and night,*
*so that you may be careful to do according to all that is written in it.*
*For then you will make your way prosperous,*
*and then you will have good success.*
(Joshua 1:8)

We have seen across the pages of *Prosper* that the "blessed man" is the one who meditates on the Word of God. *"Blessed is the man who walks not in the counsel of the wicked, nor stands in the way of sinners, nor sits in the seat of scoffers; but his delight is in the law of the Lord, and on His law he meditates day and night. He is like a tree planted by streams of water that yields its fruit in its season, and its leaf does not wither. In all that he does, he prospers"* (Psalm 1:1-3).

## WHAT IS MEDITATION?

As discussed in Chapter 5 of *Prosper*, the Hebrew word translated as *meditate* is *hagah* which could also be translated as "moan, muse, or devise." In Isaiah 31:4 this word is used to depict a young lion growling (*hagah*) over his prey. The idea is a deep-seated contemplation. The biblical definition of *meditation* is the polar opposite of the world's perspective.

The world says, "Meditate!" Empty your mind.
God says, "Meditate." Fill your mind with My Word.
The world says, "Relax your mind."
The Word says, "Focus your mind on eternal things."

## PRACTICAL MEDITATION ON GOD'S WORD

The guide I'm about to share with you is but one way to spend time in the Word of God. Over the years, I have used many techniques and formats, but I find this method exceedingly practical. It's not a perfect method, but it is a feasible way to meditate on God's Word and a good place to begin your study.

I call it **"The 20-10-5-1."**

## THE METHOD: 20-10-5-1

Whenever you open the Word of God, do so prayerfully, patiently, persistently, and purposefully.

The four components are as follows:

- **Twenty** is for **OBSERVATION.**
- **Ten** is for **INTERROGATION.**
- **Five** is for **CONTEMPLATION.**
- **One** is for **APPLICATION.**

### OBSERVATIONS FROM THE PASSAGE (20)

After prayerfully approaching the Word of God and reading the passage aloud, observe anything noteworthy about the text. By *observe*, I don't mean find some deep spiritual meaning or scrutinize the original Hebrew. Yes, there is a place and time for such study, but this exercise is to note twenty observations from a single verse or short passage.

To illustrate, if I were sitting in front of you, you would observe many things:

    1) Nate is wearing a short-sleeved shirt.
    2) He is currently barefoot.
    3) He is drinking a soy latte.
    4) He is working on a MacBook Air.
    5) He is quite bald.
    6) He is sitting in a hotel room.
    7) He is writing a book.

The list could go on.

Now go to Scripture. Take Matthew 9:37-38 as an example.

> *Then He said to His disciples, "The harvest is plentiful, but the laborers are few; therefore pray earnestly to the Lord of the harvest to send out laborers into His harvest."*

Let's make a few observations from this text.

    1) Jesus is the one **speaking** (*He said to His disciples*).
    2) There is a **surety** of a harvest (*the harvest is plentiful*).
    3) There is a **shortage** of workers in His field (*the laborers are few*).
    4) Christ's priority is for His disciples to be **seeking** Him first (*therefore pray*).
    5) The Lord's work is the **subject** of our prayers (*pray earnestly to the Lord of the harvest to send out laborers into His harvest*).
    6) Prayer is a **serious** responsibility (*pray earnestly*).
    7) God does the **sending** of workers into His field (*pray earnestly to the Lord of the harvest to send out laborers*).

Though such observations may seem mundane, as you dig into a passage in this way (not stopping after one or two observations), you will begin to think deeply on the scene that has been set, and the Holy Spirit will begin to open your mind to what He is thinking. Don't give in to the temptation to stop after a few reflections. **Find a minimum of twenty observations in each verse.** Seem impossible? It's not. A couple of friends and I found more than twenty observations in Christ's words from the cross, *"I thirst"* (John 19:28).

During this process of observation, expect to read the passage 10-15 times. Feel stuck? Read it again and again. Maybe read it in another respected version of Scripture in order to hear the same truth with slightly different wording.

Keep a journal of your observations, and you'll soon have your own commentary! After finding twenty such observations, you may want to listen to a sermon or read a commentary on the passage—and find twenty more. Better yet, invite a friend to muse on the passage with you, and keep adding to the list.

## INTERROGATION OF THE PASSAGE (10)

After finding your observations, interrogate the passage. Though the mark is set at ten questions, I usually find this to be too few.

Asking questions about the passage will feed further study (for later), connect the original passage to other passages in Scripture, and bring to light thoughts you had never considered. Be like a crime scene investigator on *Sherlock Holmes, Criminal Minds, Psyche,* or *Monk.* Ask the basic investigative questions: Who? What? Why? Where? When?

Go back to Matthew 9:37-38. Let's interrogate the passage.

- Why is Jesus speaking to His disciples?
- What does it mean that the harvest is plentiful?
- What or who is the harvest?
- Why are the laborers presently few?
- Why does Jesus call His disciples to first pray instead of saying "Go!"?
- What does it mean that Jesus is "Lord of the harvest"?
- How will we know when He sends us out into His harvest?

The questions could go on and on. As a side note, most of my sermons are born from such interrogation of a passage.

## CONTEMPLATION OF THE PASSAGE (5)

Allow me to encourage you to spend five minutes in absolute silence following your time of observation and interrogation. This silence is not for sleeping or waiting for the clock to tick 300 times. It is a time to ponder the observations and questions you have scribbled down. It is an opportunity to soak in the meditations you have had and to allow the Lord to convict you of what needs to happen next.

Good news. He will communicate His mind to you.

## APPLICATION FOR YOUR LIFE (1)

Whether I'm in a group of twenty youth or by myself, one application per person is suggested. James 1:22-25 compares the Word of God to a mirror. I don't use a mirror to clean my face or body, nor do I use it to examine others. Its purpose is to reflect my own face, that I might respond accordingly.

In the same way, when I look into the law of the Lord (God's love letter to me), I am mercifully given the opportunity to see what it exposes in my life—with the intent that I become more conformed to the image of Jesus Christ. A good question to ask ourselves as we go through our day is: How is this day different, and how have I changed as a result of marinating in God's Word?

## A BONUS

I hesitate to write this since I don't want to rob you of the delight of discovering it for yourself, but some of you might need the extra motivation, so here it is.

**I have found that there is a wonderful by-product of studying the Word of God in this manner.** Not only do you glean incalculable blessings from meditating on and marinating in God's Word, but, without trying, you memorize it as well. While I can quote hundreds of verses, the majority of the ones most deeply ingrained in my mind and heart are not the ones memorized intentionally. Many of the verses I know best entered my memory bank as a result of deeply meditating on the Word of God and hiding it in the depths of my heart.

My friends, "20-10-5-1" might sound overly simplistic, but I invite you to dive humbly and prayerfully into Scripture with this approach. Get ready for the Holy Spirit to communicate to you the things of Christ.

And, as you meditate on the Holy Scriptures, remember this: **The one who meditates day and night on the Word of God will be the one who *prospers.***

## *Appendix II*
# BIBLE MARKING & HIGHLIGHTING

Let me say this at the outset.

> **You can mark up your Bible all you want,**
> **but if you don't let your Bible mark *you*,**
> **it is a worthless practice.**

This is not about having a colorful Bible; rather, it's about having an intimate walk with Jesus Christ. Additionally, let me say that not everyone feels comfortable highlighting and making notes in their Bible, and that is fine. Think of Bible marking as a helpful tool rather than a rigid requirement. That said, **I share the following ideas because they have made a great difference in my own personal study and meditation of God's Word.**

Solomon wrote, *"If you call out for insight and raise your voice for understanding, if you seek it like silver and search for it as for hidden treasures, then you will understand the fear of the Lord and find the knowledge of God"* (Proverbs 2:3-5). There is a phrase in the 2001 movie *The Lord of the Rings: The Fellowship of the Ring* which has been made famous by memes. The character Boromir says, "One does not simply walk into Mordor." **Similarly, we can say, "One does not simply find the hidden gems of Scripture on the surface."** I am not saying that great truths cannot be quickly gleaned, but I am saying that the deeper you dig, the greater the eternal riches you will discover. Additionally, by systematic and organized highlighting, it is easier to go back and continue digging where you left off rather than starting the excavation over again.

## WHY MARK UP YOUR BIBLE?

As we discuss practical components of Bible marking, let me suggest a few reasons this can be a valuable practice:

- In my study of the Word, marking allows me **to remember things the Holy Spirit has emphasized to my mind and heart.**

- Also, it greatly helps me to **quickly reference Scriptures** when I want to go back to them.

- Finally, when teaching God's Word, I can jump from thought to thought in a succinct and organized fashion by **seeing where the connecting thoughts are found** on the page.

**Consider the way the Word of God is described.** First, it is described as a **sword**. *"For the word of God is living and active, sharper than any two-edged sword, piercing to the division of soul and of spirit, of joints and of marrow, and discerning the thoughts and intentions of the heart"* (Hebrews 4:12). A person who wishes to use a sword skillfully must be trained in swordsmanship or fencing. One is not born with such mastery. Likewise, we must be trained in the Word of God. *"All Scripture is breathed out by God and profitable for teaching, for reproof, for correction, and for training in righteousness, that the man of God may be complete, equipped for every good work"* (2 Timothy 3:16-17).

Many other analogies could be listed. The Word of God is described as a **light**. The psalmist penned, *"Your word is a lamp to my feet and a light to my path"* (Psalm 119:105). It is referenced as **nourishment** or

**bread**. *"Man shall not live by bread alone, but by every word that comes from the mouth of God"* (Matthew 4:4). Also, *"Is not my word like **fire**, declares the Lord, and like a **hammer** that breaks the rock in pieces?"* (Jeremiah 23:29). **As we dive into studying God's Word, it is helpful to understand that this is not so much about creativity as it is about intentionality.** This is about being intentional in getting to know God and in making Him known.

## THE FOUR STEPS IN BIBLE MARKING

Let's limit our Bible marking principles to four simple steps.

**(1) Plan**
**(2) Prime**
**(3) Perceive**
**(4) Preserve**

## STEP 1: PLAN

When I say *plan*, I'm not presently referring to a Bible reading plan. At various times in my life I have used Bible reading plans, but I prefer to not limit my reading to a schedule or a chapter ending. Even lovers of the Word can get discouraged when they fall behind or might simply stop because they are "done" for the day. I love being neither ahead nor behind! Rather, I take a certain allotment of time and just read Scripture, putting a bookmark where I left off. If later in the day I have more free time, why not spend some of it absorbing the Word of God?

Now if you struggle with discipline and order, then a reading plan might be the way to go. But I would suggest that you switch up the order in which you read through the Scriptures. Obviously, read the Word from front to back (Genesis to Revelation), but maybe on another occasion, read the Scriptures chronologically (the order in which the books were written or took place), or read the Old Testament in parallel with the New Testament. But be intentional and consistent as you work your way through books and passages of Scripture. Avoid randomly jumping around. And the main thing is this: **Be in the Word of God** *"day and night"* (Psalm 1:2).

Along with your systematic reading of Scripture, be prepared with tools to mark your Bible. A quick list of supplies would include:

• **A reliable translation of the Scripture** (I prefer hard copy rather than digital). Personally, I choose to use the ESV, NKJV, NLT, or the NASB. It is often useful to look at a couple English versions when doing an in-depth study as slight differences can indicate an original word with a deeper meaning. In such cases, a word study may be in order.

• **Fine-point black pens for making notes** (brands and quality change, so do your research). Some prefer to use a mechanical pencil with an eraser, allowing them to correct or fine-tune their notes along the way.

• **Set of highlighters** (that do not easily bleed through the page) with at least five different colors. Another option is to use colored pencils, sometimes preferred by those with an artistic flair.

• **A notebook** (for writing down your gleanings from the Word). You will not want to include all the notes from your notebook in the margins of your Bible. A notebook allows you to record and sort the thoughts the Holy Spirit gives you to process.

## STEP 2: PRIME

*Prime* can mean "to put liquid into a pump to seal the moving parts and facilitate the operation," or it can be a neutral color of paint you apply to a wall to get it ready for the final color. **Simply put, when you prime something, you are preparing it for greater use.** This is the idea. We want to prime the passage. How do we do that?

**DISCLAIMER:** There are many ways to begin marking a passage, and I am not claiming my method is better than another. I am simply sharing how I do it.

**GREEN**

• I begin by using a **green highlighter** and marking **all references to God** (Father, Son, and Holy Spirit). This may include pronouns along with other names of God in the passage. This is merely a priming of the passage. I want to see what God is saying, doing, asking, commanding, or teaching.

**ORANGE**

• Then, I take the **orange highlighter** and highlight **all the questions found in the passage**, whatever ends in a question mark. This allows me to identify what is being discussed.

**YELLOW**

• On most occasions, I keep my **yellow highlighter** close by since I use it **for verses and thoughts that stand out to me or remind me of a truth I need to return to often and remember.** And if there is something going on in my life at the time when this truth hits home, I take my fine-point pen and make a small note of when and how this verse impacted my life (this is part of STEP 4: PRESERVE).

**RED**

• Though this point will fall under the next category (PERCEIVE), I should mention that I use my **red highlighter** throughout Scripture for **references to the gospel (death,**

**burial, and resurrection of Christ)**. Remember that Christ can be seen in all the Scriptures (Luke 24:27), so I use this color also in the Old Testament—wherever I see pictures and prophecies that point to the Messiah and His redemptive work. Some students of the Word choose to simply draw a small cross next to such passages.

Since each book of the Bible contains different themes, I tend to make **a marking key at the start of a book, which helps me be consistent with the colors and symbols being used for each aspect.** For example, in the book of Proverbs, I may draw a small heart next to each verse which speaks of the heart, or, for every verse that contains a warning for the fool, I may put an exclamation mark by the text. Regardless, consistency is paramount in marking if you want to maintain clarity. That said, I always use green, orange, yellow, and red for the aforementioned subjects and topics.

## STEP 3: PERCEIVE

*Perceive* means to "become aware or conscious of (something); come to realize or understand." Solomon wrote, *"The Preacher sought to find words of delight, and uprightly he wrote words of truth"* (Ecclesiastes 12:10). As we study the Word of God and find such words of delight, **it is wise to stop, take note of them, and mark them for remembrance.** You can do this in the margins, in your journal, or simply in a notebook.

In the journey of perceiving, **let me emphasize that we must do this prayerfully and cautiously**. Prayerfully because, without the Spirit of God, we will be unable to understand what God wants to communicate. *"Now we have received not the spirit of the world, but the Spirit who is from God, that we might understand the things freely given us by God"* (1 Corinthians 2:12). Cautiously, because we are commanded to accurately handle *"the Word of Truth"* (2 Timothy 2:15).

There are many ways we can observe a passage, but I'll share seven angles (outside of the ones previously mentioned) that I look for. As you do a 20-10-5-1 (see Appendix I) through a passage, these aspects will become visible. These various points will be part of the key you compose at the beginning of a book.

**1. LOOK FOR REPETITION.** What is the Word of God reiterating? Perhaps you will want to highlight or underline the themes running through the passage. This repetition may be a word, phrase, character, or idea.

**2. LOOK FOR KEYWORDS.** Just as a physical key unlocks a door, keywords will be those words which unlock the meaning of the passage, the main thought being conveyed. Highlighting such words will give you a deeper understanding of what God is saying. Find the dictionary definition of the word, look up other times that same word is used in Scripture (you can do this online using a Bible search tool), and take time to investigate the word using *Strong's Concordance* (available free in many places online) to understand the Hebrew, Aramaic, or Greek word being used.

**3. LOOK FOR COMMANDS TO OBEY.** As we discovered in Chapter 9 of *Prosper*, these commands are not meant to limit our joy, but to show us His love. They are an invitation to know the heart of God. As Jesus said in John 14:21, *"Whoever has My commandments and keeps them, he it is who loves Me. And he who loves Me will be loved by My Father, and I will love him and manifest Myself to him."*

**4. LOOK FOR SINS TO AVOID.** Keep in mind that salvation is not obtained by avoiding sin but by receiving God's gift of eternal life through the finished work of Jesus Christ. As followers of Christ, our passion to avoid sin is not in order to have a relationship with God but because we have been given a relationship with Him through the Person and work of the Lord Jesus Christ (see Ephesians 2:1-10). The one who desires to walk with Jesus Christ

**4** and enjoy intimacy with Him will be looking *for anything that misses the mark* (the definition of sin). *"Since it is written, 'You shall be holy, for I am holy'"* (1 Peter 1:16).

**5** **5. LOOK FOR PROMISES OF GOD TO HOLD ONTO.** As we walk through the Word, it is important for us to build our life on the foundation which never changes. *"God is not man, that He should lie, or a son of man, that He should change His mind. Has He said, and will He not do it? Or has He spoken, and will He not fulfill it?"* (Numbers 23:19). If *"the worlds were framed by the word of God"* (Hebrews 11:3 NKJV), how much more should our lives be framed by God's Word? In times of confusion, disappointment, and discouragement, how sweet it is to walk through the Word and discover afresh those highlighted portions of God's promises.

**6** **6. LOOK FOR PEOPLE, PLACES, TIME FRAMES, AND THINGS.** Remember that *"all Scripture is breathed out by God"* (2 Timothy 3:16). These details will often link passages and reveal a deeper understanding of a passage or story. All of the Bible is ultimately one story, and oftentimes, when these ideas repeat themselves, it is a call for us to connect the dots. Connecting the dots is much easier when we can quickly go back and see the color-coordinated highlights that remind us of what was said.

**7** **7. LOOK FOR EXAMPLES TO FOLLOW AND EXAMPLES FROM WHICH TO TAKE A WARNING.** The stories of Scripture not only point us to our need for Jesus Christ, but they also direct us in the way in which we should walk. While the Bible sets before us many good examples to follow, it is also replete with bad examples to not follow. *"Now these things happened to them as an example, but they were written down for our instruction, on whom the end of the ages has come"* (1 Corinthians 10:11). We have examples recorded for us throughout the pages of Scripture, showing us how God thinks and responds to the lives of women and men. And what does

God want? The prophet Isaiah shared, *"But this is the one to whom I will look: he who is humble and contrite in spirit and trembles at My Word"* (Isaiah 66:2). In a spirit of humility and trembling, may we submit to God's Word.

**7**

**8. LOOK FOR THE DEMONSTRATION OF GOD'S CHARACTERISTICS** (mercy, love, grace, faithfulness, power, justice, etc.). We have already covered the identification of God's presence (green highlighting) on the pages of Scripture, but I would strongly encourage taking the time to separately mark God's characteristics.

**8**

## STEP 4: PRESERVE

Finally, we must preserve what we gleaned. Scripture commands us to *"Get wisdom; get insight; do not forget, and do not turn away from the words of my mouth"* (Proverbs 4:5). A subtle pitfall is that of meditating on God's Word and gleaning from its precious truths only to walk away without doing as Moses commanded the children of Israel: *"These words that I command you today shall be on your heart. You shall* **teach them diligently** *to your children, and shall* **talk of them when you sit in your house**, *and when you walk by the way, and when you lie down, and when you rise. You shall* **bind them as a sign on your hand**, *and they shall be as frontlets between your eyes. You shall* **write them on the doorposts of your house and on your gates"** (Deuteronomy 6:6-9).

I have found it helpful, while studying Scripture, to make notes in a notebook or on a piece of paper. Then, at the end of the time, I take those notes and **summarize my gleanings from that verse or passage in concise statements or brief outlines which I then neatly write out in the margins of my Bible for later reference.**

The Word of God commands us to *"Bless the Lord, O my soul, and forget not all His benefits"* (Psalm 103:2). As you walk through life guided by God's Word, there will be many moments where certain Scriptures minister to your spirit and change your course of action, attitude, or perspective. I have appreciated the simple practice of **making a small note of the date and event in the margin next to a verse that particularly impacted my life.** It serves as a memorial of thanksgiving to the Lord for meeting me at that place and time in His Word.

## FINAL THOUGHTS

Regardless of your methods of study, your time in God's Word will be a catalyst to intimately knowing and enjoying the Lord Jesus Christ in all His beauty and glory. Our preferences of reading plans, study techniques, highlighting, or note-taking may differ (and that is fine), but may we all agree on this: God does not intend for us to merely accommodate His Word. He wants it to transform us.

As we read, study, sing, meditate upon, memorize, pray through, and speak God's Word, it will be ingrained upon our heart, mind, and life. Marking Scripture will simply be a tool to help us in our daily practice as we consciously live in God's presence, dwell on His Word, and allow it (Him!) to be our focus *"day and night"* (Psalm 1:2). The reality is that *"the grass withers, the flower fades, but the word of our God will stand forever"* (Isaiah 40:8). All who choose such a life—focused on God's Word—will be *"like a tree planted by streams of water that yields its fruit in its season, and its leaf does not wither"* (Psalm 1:3), and in **all** that they do, they **will** PROSPER.

# *Endnotes*

**DAY 1**

1. This song was penned by Keith Getty and Stuart Townsend in 2005 and is entitled, *Every Promise*. To hear a recording of the song, check out Keith and Kristyn Getty's album *"Awaken the Dawn."*

**DAY 2**

2. This quote came from a message delivered by Timothy Keller on September 23, 2012, entitled "Gospel in Life: Grace in the Case of Naaman." Accessible on *Logos Software* through the Timothy Keller Sermon Archive, 2012-2013. New York: Redeemer Presbyterian Church.

3. J.H. Sammis was born in 1846 in Brooklyn, New York. At 40 years of age, Sammis wrote the beloved hymn, *Trust and Obey*. Ira D. Sankey, who ministered through music alongside the preaching ministry of Dwight L. Moody, gave us a little background to this song in his biography, *My Life and the Story of the Gospel Hymns*. Sankey noted, *"Mr. Moody was conducting a series of meetings in Brockton, Massachusetts, and I had the pleasure of singing for him there. One night a young man rose in a testimony meeting and said, 'I am not quite sure—but I am going to trust, and I am going to obey.' I just jotted that sentence down, and sent it with a little story to the Rev. J. H. Sammis, a Presbyterian minister. He wrote the hymn, and the tune was born."*

**DAY 3**

4. Eliza Edmunds Hewitt, born in Philadelphia, Pennsylvania, in 1851, suffered a severe spinal injury early in her teaching career when a student hit her across the back with a slate. It was through a journey of pain and change of lifestyle that Hewitt's poetic gift was greatly developed. This verse comes from one of her most well-beloved hymns, *My Faith Has Found a Resting Place*. Published in 1891 in *Songs of Joy and Gladness, No. 2*, this hymn is still included in many songbooks today.

**DAY 4**

5. Malcom Gladwell dives into this idea throughout his book published in 2008 by *Little, Brown, and Company*, entitled *Outliers*.

6. Originally published in French in 1692, this book, *The Practice of the Presence of God* is a series of journal entries by a priest referred to as "Brother Lawrence."

7. This song, *Linger*, is by the band *Warr Acres* from Warr Acres, Oklahoma. Released in 2013, this song appeared on their album, *Hope Will Rise*.

**DAY 5**

8. Kate Wilkinson was born in England in 1859. Kate devoted much of her time investing in young women through the Keswick Deeper Life Convention movement. Keswick, a market town and urban district in Cumberland, England, also became the place of great revival through the Keswick Convention, which continues to this day. As with any true revival, an emphasis is placed on the Word of God along with dependence and surrender to Christ. Thus, Wilkinson's hymn, born in this place, reflects the heart prepared to see a work of God. *May the Mind of Christ My Savior* was first published in the 1925 *Golden Bells Hymnal*, three years before Wilkinson's death.

**DAY 6**

9. For our mere understanding, we should note that tithing, or giving 10%, was an Old Testament practice, but as we walk into the life of the Church, the question changes. It's no longer, "What we are supposed to give?" but rather, "How much can I give?" and "How little can we live on?" Again, this is an opportunity to invest in eternity, not an obligation to give to a begging God (which is never the picture we see in Scripture). See Acts 17:24-25.

10. These statistics come from Nielsen's Total Audience Report (Q1, 2019). Take a closer look yourself to find more information on how media specifically is dominating the lives of many.

11. Written by Southern Gospel artist Kirk Talley, this song, entitled *Quiet Time*, appeared on Talley's solo album *Shhhh*. Produced by Sonlite Records, this album was released in November of 1997.

**DAY 7**

12. C.S. Lewis' essay, *Is Theology Poetry?* was first presented to the Oxford Socratic Club on November 6, 1944. Later on, this essay was included in various compilations of Lewis' writing.

13. Frances Ridley Havergal was born in England in 1836 and had a great love for learning. Despite serious health issues (she died at 42 years of age), she was proficient in Greek and Hebrew and had a gift for poetry. This particular hymn has a well-documented history as Havergal explained its background in a letter to a friend. "Perhaps you will be interested to know the origin of the consecration hymn, *Take my Life*. I went for a little visit of five days. There were ten persons in the house, some unconverted and long prayed for, some converted but not rejoicing Christians. He gave me the prayer, 'Lord, give me all in this house!' And He just did! Before I left the house, everyone had got a blessing. The last night of my visit I was too happy to sleep, and passed most of the night in praise and renewal of my own consecration, and these little couplets formed themselves and chimed in my heart one after another, till they finished with, 'Ever, ONLY, **ALL** for Thee!'"

**DAY 8**

14. Russell Kelso Carter was a man of many talents. Born in Baltimore, Maryland, in 1849, Carter was an outstanding athlete and a scholar. As a professor at the Pennsylvania Military Academy, he held teaching posts in chemistry, natural science, civil engineering, and mathematics and authored books on this subject, along with novels. If that were not enough, Carter also raised sheep and practiced medicine. It was while teaching at the military academy that Carter wrote this martial music-style hymn, *Standing on the Promises*.

**DAY 9**

15. This quote comes from Tim Keller's book, *The Prodigal God: Recovering the Heart of the Christian Faith*. First published by Penguin Group in 2008, this book is easily one of the best books I have ever read on the heart of the Gospel.

16. This William Cowper hymn was first published in *Olney Hymns* in 1779. Born in England in 1731, Cowper was educated to be an attorney, but due to his frequent bouts with depression (and even a suicide attempt), he struggled to maintain a normal life. Even his faith journey was filled with deeming himself bound for an eternity of God's wrath. A friendship with John Newton (author of *Amazing Grace*) did change the trajectory of his life as they,

together, actively opposed slavery. In fact, Cowper was often quoted by Martin Luther King Jr. during the Civil Rights Movement. How beautiful to see these lyrics, written late in his life, portraying the true freedom he experienced through the work of Jesus Christ on his behalf.

**DAY 10**

17. Philip Bliss was born in Pennsylvania in 1838 and gave his life to Christ at twelve years of age. For many years, he worked as an itinerant music instructor until Dwight L. Moody asked him to become a singing evangelist. This particular song was titled *My Prayer* and was written a mere three years (1873) before Philip Bliss and his wife tragically died in a tragin train accident.

**DAY 11**

18. Annie Hawks was a gifted songwriter who devoted her life to raising her three children. It was in her faithful care of the home that God inspired her. In Hawk's own words, *"One day as a young wife and mother of 37 years of age, I was busy with my regular household tasks during a bright June morning [in 1872]. Suddenly, I became so filled with the sense of nearness to the Master that, wondering how one could live without Him, either in joy or pain, these words were ushered into my mind, the thought at once taking full possession of me—'I Need Thee Every Hour. . ..'"* Though Hawks composed over 400 hymns, this song is the only one commonly sung today.

**DAY 12**

19. This song took on special meaning to me as I navigated cancer. Ron Hamilton wrote this song shortly after being diagnosed with cancer in his left eye. Though at the time things looked bleak, it was through this very ordeal that God opened up to the Hamilton family a lifetime of children's music ministry through "Patch the Pirate." How easy it is to discard as useless the very episodes of life which God intends for our formation. Peter the apostle said it well, *"So that the tested genuineness of your faith—more precious than gold that perishes though it is tested by fire—may be found to result in praise and glory and honor at the revelation of Jesus Christ"* (1 Peter 1:7).

**DAY 13**

20. Annie Flint Johnson was an extraordinary character. She gave her life to Christ at the age of 8 and had a passion to serve and minister to children. That said, her body failed her, and in her biography, *The Making of the Beautiful*, Roland Bingham (the author) shared how she had cancer, was incontinent, having to be helped with the most basic of human needs, and had so many boils and sores on her body from lying in bed that it took eight

pillows to cushion her. Yet this is the backdrop to the hymn so many have found comfort in. We may claim to want to know intimately the grace of God, but do we want the experiences and circumstances that accompany such a gift? While it's easy to imagine the lyrics of our favorite hymns being written in a sterile study by an inspired artist, some of the most beautiful and soothing words we sing issued from writhing, agony-filled writers. Such was the story of Annie Flint Johnson and *He Giveth More Grace.*

### DAY 14

21. Written around 1924 by Kitty Louise Suffield, this song has an amazing story behind it. Robert J. Morgan, in his book *Then Sings My Soul,* shares many of the details. "One snow-blanketed night, Canadian Fred Suffield awoke to an urgent pounding on his door. A half-frozen man reported that a train had stalled in the blizzard, and the passengers were in danger of freezing to death. Lighting a lantern, Fred followed the man to the site and led the travelers back to his house. Later one of the passengers, Kittie, wrote a thank you note. Fred replied, and Kittie wrote back. Their correspondence led to courtship and to marriage." But the story doesn't end there. Fred and Kittie took a young man into their home for a month of discipleship as they participated in evangelistic meetings in their hometown. With their encouragement, the young man shared a song at one of these meetings, but his voice cracked, he was mortified, and he vowed to never again sing publicly. Kittie encouraged the boy to change the key and to keep using his voice for the Lord. The young man? George Beverly Shea. Due to Shea's partnership in ministry with Billy Graham, it is safely estimated that he sang before more people than any other human in world history. Truly, Kittie's life preached the message, *Little is much when God is in it!*

### DAY 15

22. Written by Australian songwriter Colin Buchanan, this little chorus became well-known to me as a young boy attending a summer camp in Dahlonega, Georgia. Buchanan is a nine-time Golden Guitar-winning singer/songwriter and is, according to his website, Australia's #1 Christian kids' artist. You can find more of his resources at **colinbuchanan.com.au**

### DAY 16

23. Written by Mary Maxwell and published in 1900, little is recorded concerning the background to this song. That said, a channel connects two places, people, or things. It can be a water channel, a national representative who is the conduit between nations, or a wire, hose, etc. which carries resources between two things. What a beautiful prayer is echoed in

the third stanza of this song, *"Emptied that Thou shouldest fill me, a clean vessel in Thine hand, with no strength but as Thou givest, graciously with each command."*

**DAY 17**

24. Though we could go to many places to learn the purposes of root systems, I used the National Arboretum as my source. If you're interested in learning more, they have a plethora of articles and information on their website: https://www.usna.usda.gov/

25. These lyrics come from a hymn entitled, *I Wake Up This Morning, Lord.* No information on the author is available, but the lyrics to all seven verses are on **hymnal.net.**

**DAY 18**

26. The statistics of the Redwood trees are broadly documented, but if you want to find out more on the root systems of these impressive trees, check out the United States National Park Service (Redwood National Park): **https://www.nps.gov/redw/index.htm**

27. In fact, the most deep-seated taproot ever recorded was found on a wild fig tree in Echo Caves, near Ohrigstad, Transvaal, South Africa. Its roots went down 400 feet (nearly 122 meters). As a measure of comparison, that distance is greater than the length of any official-sized football (soccer) pitch.

28. *Biosphere 2* (since it was intended to be the second fully self-sufficient biosphere, after the Earth itself) was originally constructed between 1987 and 1991 in Oracle, Arizona. The structure is massive at 3.14 acres. In fact, it remains (at the time of writing) the largest closed system created. It has seven biomes, including a rainforest, an ocean with a coral reef, mangrove wetlands, savannah grassland, and a fog desert. Though *Biosphere 2* was only used twice for its intended research as a closed experiment, it continues to serve as a research tool through the University of Arizona. For more, check out the website: **biosphere2.org**

29. This song by Esther Kerr Rusthoi is one of my favorites, not *merely* for the lyrics, but for the fact that my mother would share these lyrics with me during my years of ministry in North Africa and the Middle East. When times were difficult, she would gently remind me in writing, "Nathan, it will be worth it all, when we see Jesus."

**DAY 19**

30. There is a beautiful (and tragic) story behind this Philip Bliss hymn. Dwight L. Moody was preaching at a meeting where Philip Bliss listened intently. He told of a ship approaching the Cleveland Harbor on a stormy and starless night. The lighthouse was in view. It had a lower light on the shore that was aligned with the lighthouse and which marked the passage for ships to safely make their way into the harbor, avoiding the treacherous rocks. On that particular night, however, the lower light had gone out. When the Captain asked where the lower lights were, the pilot said, "Gone out, sir." That night, the wind, waves, and currents were particularly ferocious. With the understanding that the ship would not answer to her helm, at this point, the pilot declared, "We must or we perish, sir!" Despite the strong heart and brave hand of the pilot, he missed the channel, crashing the ship onto the rocks, where it quickly sank, taking many a sailor to their watery grave. Moody made the application that Christ is the lighthouse but that He has positioned us on the shores of this world to guide wanderers home, to be the lower lights that others may look to and see the way. Bliss didn't miss the opportunity. Picking up his pen, he wrote a song treasured still today. The admonition is clear, my friends. The consequences and repercussions for not sharing and showing the gospel are not minimal. Indeed, the eternity of souls is at stake. May these words, first published in 1871, resonate in our hearts today as we seek to burn brightly in order to point souls to Christ.

**DAY 20**

31. *Love Divine All Loves Excelling* was first published in 1747. Charles Wesley, who wrote the hymn, was said to be inspired by a contemporary song of the day, *Fairest isle, all isles excelling*. Penned by John Dryden for Act 2 of Henry Purcell's opera *King Arthur* (1691), Wesley's opening lines mirror Dryden's. But the inspiration doesn't stop there. Wesley closes the hymn with *"Changed from glory into glory till in heaven we take our place, till we cast our crowns before Thee, lost in wonder, love, and praise."* Another hymnist, Joseph Addison, had written *Hymn on Gratitude to the Deity*, which closes with, *"When all thy mercies, O my God, my rising soul surveys, transported with the view, I'm lost in wonder, love, and praise."* Regardless of the background to the hymn, this song marvelously conveys the preciousness of God's work in our lives.

**DAY 21**

32. Elisha Hoffman may be better known for his hymns *Leaning on the Everlasting Arms* and *Are You Washed in the Blood?* than the one quoted here. In fact, Hoffman penned over 2,000 songs in his lifetime and often composed the music as well. That said, this song, *Is Your All on the Altar?* beautifully portrays the call to surrender our everything to Christ.

**DAY 22**

33. Laila Morris was a native of Ohio who spent nearly her whole life in that state. She wrote over 1,000 songs, many while going about her daily activities of housework. In her early fifties, Morris's eyesight began failing, so her son constructed a twenty-eight foot blackboard with oversized staff lines so that his mother could continue to minister through writing. Today, we continue to be blessed by her investment with the pen.

**DAY 23**

34. Though relatively little is written on Bryan Jeffrey Leech, he was born in Middlesex, England, in 1931. After coming to the United States, he studied at Barrington College and North Park Seminary before being ordained and ministering at First Covenant Church in Oakland, California. It wasn't until his mid-thirties that he recognized his gift for writing. Over his lifetime, he composed over 500 hymns. In his obituary (Leech died in 2015), it was noted that a love for the church was his inspiration for writing songs.

**DAY 24**

35. Born in Switzerland, Johann Kaspar Lavater became an ordained minister and carried out much of his work in Zürich (where he was born and died). His work was translated from German, and, though largely unknown, the depth of his thoughts have impacted many. He died during a period of the French Revolution when French military commander, Masséna, entered Zürich and Lavater was shot by a French grenadier. As a result of the wound, he died two months later.

**DAY 25**

36. Fred Pratt Green was born in Liverpool, England, in 1903. After serving in England as a circuit minister, along with holding various offices in the Methodist Church, Pratt turned to songwriting. He was honored as a Fellow of The Hymn Society, and, soon after his 90th birthday, he received the rare privilege of being honored by the Queen for his service in writing hymns. In 2000, he died in his sleep at the age of ninety-seven.

**DAY 26**

37. The article, "Promise-Keeping: A Low Priority in a Hierarchy of Workplace Values," was written by Ellwood F. Oakley III and Patricia Lynch and was published in the *Journal of Business Ethics*. Vol. 27, No. 4 (Oct., 2000), pp. 377-392.

38. This song is appropriately entitled *Psalm 1*, and the words are attributed to Ken Bible. Published in 1835, it falls under the CCLI Song reference #7111424.

**DAY 27**

39. Walter Smith, born in Scotland in 1824, was an ordained minister for most of his life. This song was published in 1876 in *Hymns of Christ and the Christian Life*.

**DAY 28**

40. Joachim Neander was born in Germany in 1650. At sixteen, Joachim entered the Gymnasium illustre (Academic Gymnasium) of Bremen but carried on a riotous and carefree life consumed with questionable pleasures and company. In 1670, Neander and some of his friends attended St. Martin's Church for a Sunday service in order to criticize and mock the preaching of the Word. The contrary happened. God began to grip Neander's heart, and soon after he gave his life to Christ. Though much could be said about Neander, it is important to realize that his writings came about as a result of misunderstanding from others and social rejection. Neander took a stand on many practices he deemed unbiblical, but, through this journey of being ostracized, he was drawn into a deeper relationship with the One *"who with His love doth befriend thee."*

**DAY 29**

41. François de Salignac de la Mothe-Fénelon was a French archbishop, poet, and writer. He is well known for his book, *Let Go*, along with *The Adventures of Telemachus (Les aventures de Télémaque)*.

42. The text of this hymn was written by Mary Jane (Jennie) Bain Wilson. Born in 1856 (though some sources say 1857) on a farm in Cleveland, Indiana, Wilson knew about change and trials. Her father died when she was four years of age, and she had a spinal infection that resulted in her being an invalid bound to a wheelchair. Due to not being able to attend regular school, she studied at home and became an avid reader and fell in love with music and poetry. At the age of twenty-five, Wilson was baptized by being carried in a chair into a stream. She said of that day, *"It gave me much joy to thus confess my dear Savior."* Notably, though she wrote over 2,000 songs and poems, she refused to interject sadness into her writing with an exception or two. She composed this particular poem (later a song) to reveal the contrast between life's changing landscape and eternity's sure promises.

**DAY 30**

43. Charles Austin Miles was born in 1868. Though starting out as a pharmacist, Miles spent much of his life as editor and manager at Hall-Mack publishers. The song *In the Garden* was published in 1912 and became well

known during the days of Billy Sunday's evangelistic meetings. Interestingly, according to Miles' great-granddaughter, this song was composed not in a garden but *"in a cold, dreary, and leaky basement in Pitman, New Jersey, that didn't even have a window in it let alone a view of a garden."* How good to know that the invitation to sweet communion with God is not limited by our surroundings. The garden of intimacy is available from a hospital bed, a jail cell, an office cubicle, or the comfort of our home.

**DAY 31**

44. Bruce A. Ware is a Professor of Christian Theology at the Southern Baptist Theological Seminary. He is the author of numerous journal articles, book chapters, and book reviews. Some of his more well-known works include *God's Lesser Glory; God's Greater Glory* and *Father, Son, and Holy Spirit.* Published by Crossway in 2012, *The Man Christ Jesus* focuses on the beauty of seeing Christ Jesus as fully God and fully man.

45. Born in 1850 in Dublin, Ireland, Manie Payne Ferguson moved to Los Angeles, California, with her husband where they founded the Los Angeles Mission, later renamed Peniel Mission. Though Ferguson wrote many poems and songs in her life, she is most known for the hymns *Blessed Quietness* and this one, *Man of Calvary.*